7 DAYS TO
MASTER
MANIFESTING

with 369 Manifestation Method, Law of Attraction, and Angel Numbers

WHERE THE POWER OF THOUGHT MEETS
INFINITE POSSIBILITIES

Izumi Nagi *Publications*

Discover the Ultimate
ANGEL NUMBERS *Guide*

Over **50** Pages of Insight and Guidance!

Scan the QR code to download your exclusive **Angel Numbers Guide**. Discover the meanings behind divine patterns and learn how to align with their guidance to manifest your dreams. Don't miss this powerful resource!

Your journey to clarity and transformation starts here!

Stay Focused and Organized on Your Manifestation Journey!

Scan the QR code to download your Printable Templates for Daily Manifestation Tracking.

These tools are designed to help you:

- Track your affirmations morning, afternoon, and evening.
- Monitor your progress throughout the 7-day program.
- Reflect on your daily thoughts, actions, and results.

Take the first step toward manifesting your dreams with clarity and purpose! ✦

Table of Contents

INTRODUCTION 5

CHAPTER 1: PROJECT 369 7
- The Genius Behind the Numbers: Nikola Tesla and His Legacy 7
- The Symbolism of 3, 6, and 9 7
- Practical Exercise: Starting Your 369 Journey 9
- Real-Life Stories of Success with Project 369 12

CHAPTER 2: UNDERSTANDING ANGEL NUMBERS 19
- Interpreting Angel Numbers: A Guide to Their Meanings 19
- The Spiritual Significance of Common Angel Numbers 22
- Trusting Your Intuition with Angel Numbers 30
- Real-Life Stories of Angel Number Guidance 31
- Beyond Repeated Numbers: The Full Spectrum of Angel Numbers 35
- Expand Your Knowledge with a Comprehensive Guide 38

CHAPTER 3: THE LAW OF ATTRACTION EXPLAINED 39
- Creating a Mental and Visual Vision Board 42
- Real-Life Stories of Manifestation 48

CHAPTER 4: THE POWER OF THOUGHT 52
- Shifting from Limiting to Empowering Beliefs 54
- Rewriting Negative Thought Patterns 55
- Techniques for Positive Thinking 58

CHAPTER 5: THE 7-DAY MANIFESTATION ROUTINE 69
- Day 1: Clarity of Desire 69
- Day 2: Gratitude and Abundance 73
- Day 3: Releasing Limiting Beliefs 76
- Day 4: Emotional Resonance 80
- Day 5: Inspired Action 84
- Day 6: Synchronicities and Signs 88
- Day 7: Trust and Surrender 92

CHAPTER 8: EXPANDING YOUR MANIFESTATION POWER 97

CONCLUSION 103

Introduction

What is Manifestation and Why Does It Work?

Manifestation is a concept that bridges the gap between thought, energy, and reality.

At its core, it suggests that your thoughts, beliefs, and intentions can shape the world around you. While this might sound mystical or abstract, manifestation has roots in both ancient philosophies and modern scientific understanding, particularly in the fields of psychology, quantum physics, and energy dynamics. Let's delve into what manifestation truly means, why it works, and how Project 369 and angel numbers play a crucial role in unlocking its full potential.

THE BASICS OF MANIFESTATION

Manifestation begins with the idea that everything in the universe is made up of energy, vibrating at different frequencies. This includes not only physical objects but also your thoughts, emotions, and intentions. When you focus your energy on a specific goal or desire, you align your vibration with that of the desired outcome, creating a path for it to materialize in your life.

This process doesn't happen by chance; it's the result of intentional thought, belief, and action.

Your thoughts are the starting point of manifestation. They create a blueprint for the reality you wish to experience. However, not all thoughts are created equal.

THE CONNECTION TO PROJECT 369

The Project 369 method, inspired by Nikola Tesla's fascination with the numbers 3, 6, and 9, provides a structured approach to manifestation. Tesla believed these numbers held the key to understanding the universe's energy and vibration. In the context of manifestation, these numbers represent the repetition and rhythm necessary to align your thoughts and intentions with the outcomes you desire.

THE ROLE OF ANGEL NUMBERS

Angel numbers, such as 111, 222, or 333, are sequences believed to carry messages from the universe or spiritual guides. These numbers often appear when you're aligned with your path or when guidance is needed. For example, seeing 111 might indicate that your thoughts are manifesting quickly, urging you to maintain positivity.

Why 7 Days?

The concept of dedicating 7 days to mastering manifestation isn't arbitrary; it's deeply rooted in both spiritual traditions and modern psychology. Seven days symbolize a perfect cycle—enough time to focus your energy, reprogram your mindset, and initiate real change. Let's explore why this time frame is significant and how it aligns with universal principles, personal growth, and practical application.

Chapter 1: Project 369

The Genius Behind the Numbers: Nikola Tesla and His Legacy

Nikola Tesla, the visionary inventor and physicist, is widely regarded as one of the greatest minds of the modern age. Best known for his contributions to the development of alternating current (AC) power systems and wireless communication, Tesla's genius extended far beyond conventional science. He often spoke of the profound significance of numbers, particularly 3, 6, and 9, hinting that these figures held the key to unlocking the universe's mysteries.

Tesla's Fascination with Numbers

Why these numbers? Tesla noticed that 3, 6, and 9 appeared repeatedly in nature, geometry, and even human behavior. He saw them as a kind of universal code, a language through which the cosmos expresses itself. Tesla reportedly designed his life around these numbers, often performing actions in sets of three, whether it was knocking on a door three times or circling a building three times before entering. To him, this wasn't superstition—it was a deliberate effort to harmonize with the energy of the universe.

The Symbolism of 3, 6, and 9

The numbers 3, 6, and 9 have long been associated with profound spiritual and metaphysical significance. Nikola Tesla wasn't the first to observe their unique properties, but his belief in their "magnificence" has inspired countless individuals to explore their deeper meanings. These numbers are often regarded as a key to understanding creation, harmony, and the interconnected nature of existence. Let's delve into what each number represents and why they hold such power.

The Power of 3: Creation and Expression

The number 3 is universally recognized as a symbol of creation, communication, and growth. It is often referred to as the number of the divine, reflecting the interplay between the spiritual, mental, and physical realms.

The Balance of 6: Harmony and Relationships

The number 6 is often associated with balance, love, and nurturing. It represents the harmonious connection between the spiritual and material worlds, urging us to create stability in our lives.

The Completion of 9: Spiritual Awakening

The number 9 is the culmination of the cycle, representing completion, enlightenment, and higher consciousness. In numerology, it is considered the most evolved number, symbolizing a deeper understanding of the universe

The Interplay Between 3, 6, and 9

What makes these numbers so remarkable is how they interact with each other. Together, they form a cohesive system that reflects the natural rhythms of the universe:

- ✓ **3 as the Foundation:** The initial spark of intention and creation.
- ✓ **6 as the Bridge:** The harmonizer that connects the intention to action.
- ✓ **9 as the Completion:** The point where energy cycles back, bringing your manifestations to life.

This sequence mirrors the creative process in everything, from the growth of a plant to the completion of a project. It begins with an idea, transitions through a phase of nurturing, and culminates in a fully realized outcome.

Practical Exercise: Starting Your 369 Journey

Step 1: Define Your Goal

Ask Yourself the Right Questions:

- What do I truly want to manifest in my life?
- How will achieving this goal make me feel?
- What specific outcomes do I want to see?

Write It Down: Use a journal or notebook to describe your goal in detail. Be as specific as possible. For example, instead of writing, "I want to be happy," try, "I am so grateful for my new job, where I feel fulfilled, supported, and energized every day."

Choose a Single Focus: While it's tempting to work on multiple goals at once, it's best to focus on one specific intention during your initial 7-day journey. This allows you to channel your energy and attention effectively.

Step 2: Craft Your Affirmation

Once you've defined your goal, create a powerful affirmation that aligns with your intention. Remember, your affirmation should be positive, present-tense, and emotionally charged.

Formula for an Effective Affirmation:

- Start with gratitude: *"I am so grateful for..."*
- Use the present tense: Speak as if the goal has already been achieved.
- Include emotions: Describe how achieving the goal makes you feel.

Examples of Affirmations:

- "I am so grateful for my vibrant health and the energy I feel every day."

- "I am so thankful for the financial freedom I have, earning $10,000 a month doing work I love."
- "I am so happy and grateful for the loving, supportive relationships in my life."

Write your chosen affirmation in your journal. This will be the foundation of your 369 practice.

Step 3: Morning Practice (3 Times)

Each morning, shortly after waking up, write your affirmation three times. This sets the tone for your day and anchors your intention in your subconscious mind.

How to Do It:

- Find a quiet space where you won't be interrupted.
- Write your affirmation three times in your journal. As you write, visualize your goal as if it's already achieved.
- Focus on the emotions of gratitude, joy, and excitement.

Example:
If your affirmation is, *"I am so grateful for my dream job where I feel fulfilled and inspired every day,"* write it three times with full attention and emotion.

Step 4: Afternoon Practice (6 Times)

Around midday, take a few minutes to refocus your energy by writing your affirmation six times. This reinforces your intention and keeps your vibration aligned with your goal.

How to Do It:

- Choose a moment during your lunch break or a pause in your day.
- Write your affirmation six times, fully immersing yourself in the feelings associated with your desire.

- If you notice distractions or doubts, gently redirect your focus to your affirmation.

Pro Tip: Use this time to reflect on any signs or synchronicities you've noticed during the day, such as angel numbers or unexpected opportunities.

Step 5: Evening Practice (9 Times)

Before bed, complete your day by writing your affirmation nine times. This practice solidifies your intention and allows your subconscious mind to work on your goal while you sleep.

How to Do It:

- Find a peaceful space and create a calming atmosphere (e.g., light a candle or play soft music).
- Write your affirmation nine times, focusing on the sense of fulfillment and gratitude you feel.
- End with a positive statement such as, *"I trust the universe to bring my desires to me in the perfect time and way."*

Step 6: Reflect and Adjust

At the end of each day, spend a few minutes reflecting on your progress. Journaling your thoughts and observations helps you stay connected to your practice.

Questions to Reflect On:

- How did I feel during my practice today?
- Did I notice any signs or synchronicities?
- What challenges did I encounter, and how can I address them?

Make Adjustments if Needed: If you feel disconnected or unfocused, try experimenting with different techniques, such as adding visualization or gratitude exercises to your routine.

Real-Life Stories of Success with Project 369

Stories of success serve as powerful reminders of what's possible with consistent practice and belief. The Project 369 Method has transformed lives by helping people manifest their goals and align their energy with their deepest desires. This chapter highlights real-life examples of individuals who have used this method to bring their dreams to life. Each story is a testament to the power of thought, repetition, and unwavering faith in the process.

Manifesting Career Breakthroughs

Case Study: Sarah's Dream Job

Sarah was a marketing professional who felt stuck in her career. She had always dreamed of working for a creative agency where she could express her artistic talents, but fear and self-doubt held her back. After discovering the Project 369 Method, Sarah decided to give it a try.

Her Affirmation: "I am so grateful for my dream job at a creative agency, where I feel inspired and valued every day."

Her Process: Sarah wrote her affirmation three times in the morning, six times in the afternoon, and nine times at night. Each time, she visualized herself walking into her ideal workplace, collaborating with passionate colleagues, and feeling fulfilled.

The Outcome: Within three weeks, Sarah noticed a shift in her energy. She received an unexpected call from a recruiter about a role at a leading creative agency. After a smooth interview process, she landed the job. Sarah credits her success to her consistent practice and the alignment it created with her goals.

Attracting Financial Abundance

Case Study: James' Financial Freedom

James had been struggling with debt for years, feeling overwhelmed and unsure of how to improve his financial situation. When he learned about Project 369, he decided to focus on manifesting financial freedom.

His Affirmation: "I am so thankful for my financial freedom and the abundance that flows into my life effortlessly."

His Process: James made it a daily ritual to write his affirmations and visualize himself living a debt-free life. He also took inspired actions, such as budgeting and exploring new income streams.

The Outcome: Over the course of two months, James experienced a series of unexpected financial windfalls, including a significant bonus at work and the discovery of a side business opportunity that quickly became profitable. His debt was paid off within six months, and he continued using the method to grow his savings.

Improving Relationships

Case Study: Emma's Reconnection with Her Partner

Emma and her partner had been experiencing communication issues that created distance in their relationship. She felt frustrated and longed to restore the closeness they once shared.

Her Affirmation: "I am so grateful for the loving and open communication I share with my partner, which strengthens our bond every day."

Her Process: Emma incorporated the Project 369 Method into her daily routine. She also focused on improving her own communication skills and showing appreciation for her partner.

The Outcome: Within weeks, Emma noticed positive changes in her relationship. Her partner became more receptive, and their conversations grew more meaningful. The two reconnected on a deeper level, and their relationship flourished.

Health and Wellbeing Transformations

Case Study: Amanda's Recovery Journey

Amanda had been dealing with chronic fatigue for years, struggling to maintain her energy and focus. She decided to use the Project 369 Method to improve her health and wellbeing.

Her Affirmation: "I am so grateful for my vibrant health, abundant energy, and the ability to live fully every day."

Her Process: Amanda wrote her affirmations with intense emotion, visualizing herself feeling strong, energetic, and full of life. She also made small lifestyle changes, such as incorporating healthier meals and regular exercise.

The Outcome: Over time, Amanda's energy levels began to improve. She felt more motivated to care for her body and mind, which accelerated her recovery. Today, Amanda enjoys an active lifestyle and continues to use the method for ongoing wellbeing.

Creating Opportunities and Synchronicities

Case Study: Ethan's Unexpected Travel Opportunity

Ethan had always dreamed of traveling to Japan but felt it was out of reach due to financial constraints. Using the Project 369 Method, he focused on manifesting an opportunity to visit.

His Affirmation: "I am so happy and grateful for my amazing trip to Japan, where I explore and experience new adventures."

His Process: Ethan wrote his affirmations daily, visualizing himself walking through cherry blossom-lined streets and enjoying authentic Japanese cuisine. He remained open to unexpected opportunities.

The Outcome: A few months later, Ethan won a travel contest that included an all-expenses-paid trip to Japan. The synchronicity amazed him and reinforced his belief in the power of manifestation.

Career and Financial Growth

Case Study: Manifesting a Dream Job

Challenge: Emma had been stuck in a job she disliked, feeling underappreciated and unfulfilled. She wanted to transition into a creative field but doubted her abilities.

How She Used Project 369: Emma wrote the following affirmation daily:

- Morning: *"I am grateful to work as a designer in a role that values my creativity."*
- Afternoon: *"I feel excited and fulfilled as I contribute my creative talents to a supportive team."*
- Evening: *"I am so thankful for my amazing design job that allows me to express my creativity and grow professionally."* She also took inspired actions, such as updating her portfolio and applying to roles that matched her vision.

Result: Within three months, Emma was offered a job at a design agency, perfectly aligned with her affirmation. She credits her consistent belief and daily focus for this outcome.

Case Study: Attracting Financial Abundance

Challenge: Michael, a freelance consultant, struggled with inconsistent income and financial anxiety.

How He Used Project 369: Michael crafted affirmations around abundance:

- Morning: *"I am grateful for my thriving consultancy and steady flow of high-paying clients."*
- Afternoon: *"I feel confident and secure as I attract financial opportunities effortlessly."*
- Evening: *"I am so thankful for the financial freedom I now enjoy."*
  He also networked actively and expanded his services to meet market demands.

Result: Over six months, Michael doubled his client base and saw his income stabilize at levels he hadn't imagined possible.

Strengthening Relationships

Case Study: Healing a Strained Partnership

Challenge: Sarah and her partner had been experiencing communication issues and emotional distance. She wanted to rebuild trust and connection.

How She Used Project 369: Sarah focused on affirmations like:

- Morning: *"I am grateful for open and loving communication with my partner."*
- Afternoon: *"I feel supported and connected in my relationship."*
- Evening: *"I am so thankful for the harmony and joy in our partnership."* She also initiated meaningful conversations and planned quality time together.

Result: Within a month, Sarah noticed a significant improvement in their communication, and they began working as a team to address their issues.

Case Study: Attracting a Soulmate

Challenge: Brian wanted to find a life partner but felt discouraged after years of unsuccessful dating.

How He Used Project 369: His affirmations included:

- Morning: *"I am grateful for a loving and supportive partner who shares my values."*
- Afternoon: *"I feel joyful and fulfilled in a relationship built on trust and love."*
- Evening: *"I am so thankful for the soulmate I have welcomed into my life."* Brian also focused on personal growth and joined social groups to expand his network.

Result: Within six months, Brian met someone who embodied everything he had visualized, and their relationship blossomed naturally.

Improving Health and Wellness

Case Study: Overcoming Chronic Fatigue

Challenge: Lisa had been struggling with low energy and chronic fatigue, which affected her quality of life.

How She Used Project 369: Her affirmations revolved around health and vitality:

- Morning: *"I am grateful for my vibrant health and boundless energy."*
- Afternoon: *"I feel strong, energetic, and full of life."*
- Evening: *"I am so thankful for the vitality and wellness I now experience every day."* Lisa combined these affirmations with healthier habits, including regular exercise and balanced nutrition.

Result: Over several weeks, she experienced noticeable improvements in her energy levels and overall well-being.

Case Study 6: Manifesting Weight Loss

Challenge:
Kevin wanted to lose weight but struggled with motivation and consistency.

How He Used Project 369: Kevin crafted affirmations such as:

- Morning: *"I am grateful for my healthy and fit body."*
- Afternoon: *"I feel motivated and inspired to make choices that support my health."*
- Evening: *"I am so thankful for the strength and confidence I feel in my body."* He also implemented small, manageable changes, like preparing healthy meals and taking daily walks.

Result: Over a few months, Kevin lost 20 pounds and reported feeling happier and more confident.

Chapter 2: Understanding Angel Numbers

Angel numbers are more than just patterns of repeating digits that catch your eye — they are thought to be messages from the universe, delivered through subtle yet intentional synchronicities. These sequences, such as 111, 222, or 333, carry spiritual significance and serve as gentle nudges from your higher self or spiritual guides. They remind you that you're connected to a greater universal energy, guiding you toward alignment with your life's purpose.

How Angel Numbers Communicate with You

Angel numbers don't shout — they whisper. They appear in places you might not expect, such as:

- **Clocks and Timers:** You glance at your phone and see 11:11 or 2:22.
- **Receipts and Bills:** A total of $33.33 or an invoice number ending in 444.
- **License Plates and Addresses:** Spotting a car with the number 555 or living at an address containing 777.
- **Random Appearances:** Page numbers in books, follower counts on social media, or even the number of likes on a post.

The more you tune in, the more you realize these occurrences are not coincidences. They're intentional messages designed to catch your attention in meaningful moments.

Interpreting Angel Numbers: A Guide to Their Meanings

Every number has an energetic frequency that influences its spiritual meaning. In numerology, numbers are seen as symbolic representations of universal truths, each carrying distinct characteristics and messages. When these numbers appear in repetitive sequences, their energy is amplified, creating a powerful message from the universe.

Single Digits (0-9): Each number has a foundational meaning that can help you interpret angel numbers. For example:

    1: New beginnings, independence, and manifestation.

    2: Balance, partnerships, and harmony.

    3: Creativity, communication, and growth.

Repeating Numbers: Sequences like 111, 222, or 333 magnify the energy of their core number, emphasizing their message.

Mixed Numbers: Combinations like 123 or 456 often signify progress, alignment, or steps toward a goal.

Decoding Repeating Angel Numbers

Here's a breakdown of some of the most common angel numbers and their meanings:

111: Aligning Thoughts with Reality. This number is a powerful reminder that your thoughts create your reality. Seeing 111 often means your thoughts are manifesting rapidly, so it's essential to focus on positivity and intention.

- *Message:* Stay mindful of what you're thinking about, as the universe is amplifying your energy.

222: Trust and Balance. When you see 222, it's a sign to trust the process and have faith in your journey. This number often appears when you need reassurance that everything is unfolding as it should.

- *Message:* Seek balance in your relationships and decisions, and trust that you're on the right path.

333: Spiritual Growth and Support. This number signifies that your spiritual guides are close, offering encouragement and support. It's a call to embrace your creative potential and align with your higher purpose.

- *Message:* You are being guided toward growth and self-expression —trust in the process.

444: Protection and Stability. When 444 appears, it's a sign that you're protected and supported by higher forces. This number often comes during challenging times, reminding you to stay grounded and confident.

- *Message:* You are not alone —your spiritual guides are watching over you.

555: Embracing Change. The number 555 signals transformation and new opportunities. It encourages you to let go of old patterns and embrace the changes that will lead to growth.

- *Message:* Change is necessary for progress; trust that these shifts will bring positive outcomes.

666: Rebalancing Priorities. Often misunderstood, 666 is not a negative number but a gentle nudge to reassess your focus. It reminds you to balance material concerns with spiritual alignment.

- *Message:* Align your thoughts and actions with your highest values.

777: Divine Alignment and Luck. Seeing 777 is a sign of spiritual alignment and divine support. It often appears when you're on the brink of a breakthrough or spiritual awakening.

- *Message:* Trust that you're aligned with your soul's purpose and that blessings are on their way.

888: Abundance and Success. This number signifies financial and material abundance, as well as recognition for your efforts. It's a powerful reminder that the universe rewards persistence and faith.

- *Message:* Embrace the flow of abundance in your life and keep working toward your goals.

999: Completion and Transition. The number 999 symbolizes the end of a cycle and the beginning of a new phase. It encourages you to release the past and embrace the opportunities that await.

- *Message:* Let go of what no longer serves you and make room for new beginnings.

Interpreting Mixed Angel Numbers

Mixed sequences, such as 123 or 456, can have layered meanings that relate to progress, steps, or sequences in your life journey. For example:

123: Simplify your life and take the next logical steps toward your goals.

456: You are moving in the right direction —keep building on your current momentum.

747: Your spiritual journey is aligning with divine timing, and you're being guided.

When interpreting mixed numbers, consider the core meanings of each digit and how they interact in the sequence.

The Spiritual Significance of Common Angel Numbers

111: Manifestation and Alignment

The number 111 is often the first angel number people notice, and for good reason. It signals that your thoughts are aligning with the universal energy, amplifying their potential to manifest into reality.

- **Key Message:** Be mindful of your thoughts. The universe is attuned to your energy and bringing your focus into reality.

- **Spiritual Meaning:** New beginnings, manifestation, and self-awareness.
- **When You See It:** Pause and evaluate your current thoughts. Are they aligned with your desires, or are they rooted in fear or doubt? Shift your focus to positivity and intention.

Example: If you're starting a new project and see 111, it's a sign to trust your instincts and take bold action.

222: Balance and Trust

The number 222 encourages you to find balance in your life and trust that everything is unfolding as it should. It often appears when you're working through relationships or partnerships, signaling harmony and cooperation.

- **Key Message:** Trust the process. The universe is aligning things in your favor, even if the results aren't immediately visible.
- **Spiritual Meaning:** Balance, patience, and cooperation.
- **When You See It:** Focus on maintaining inner harmony and trusting the timing of your life.

Example: Seeing 222 during a challenging time in a relationship is a reminder to approach the situation with patience and understanding.

333: Spiritual Support and Growth

When you see 333, it's a message from your spiritual guides that they are near, offering encouragement and support. It's a call to embrace your creative and spiritual potential.

- **Key Message:** You're not alone. Trust in the guidance of your spiritual team as you navigate growth and transformation.
- **Spiritual Meaning:** Divine support, creativity, and alignment with your purpose.
- **When You See It:** Take inspired action toward your goals, knowing that you are supported by the universe.

Example: If you're contemplating a major life change, 333 serves as a reassurance that you're on the right path and have the universe's backing.

444: Protection and Stability

The number 444 is a sign of protection and grounding. It often appears during times of uncertainty, reminding you that you are safe, supported, and exactly where you need to be.

- **Key Message:** Stay grounded and trust that you are protected.
- **Spiritual Meaning:** Stability, protection, and foundation.
- **When You See It:** Focus on building strong foundations in your life, whether in relationships, career, or personal growth.

Example: Seeing 444 when considering a new business venture is a sign to proceed confidently, knowing you're being guided.

555: Transformation and Opportunity

The appearance of 555 signals that significant changes are on the horizon. While change can feel daunting, this number assures you that transformation is necessary for growth and aligns you with your higher purpose.

- **Key Message:** Embrace the changes ahead with confidence and trust that they are leading you to something greater.
- **Spiritual Meaning:** Transformation, adaptability, and new opportunities.
- **When You See It:** Let go of resistance and welcome the shifts happening in your life.

Example: If you've been contemplating a move to a new city, 555 might appear as confirmation that this change will lead to positive outcomes.

666: Recalibration and Alignment

Despite its reputation, 666 is a gentle reminder to recalibrate your focus. It encourages you to balance your material concerns with spiritual priorities and realign with your higher self.

- **Key Message:** Find balance between the physical and spiritual aspects of your life.
- **Spiritual Meaning:** Realignment, balance, and grounding.
- **When You See It:** Take a moment to reflect on your current actions and adjust them to better align with your goals and values.

Example: If you're feeling overwhelmed by financial stress, 666 reminds you to focus on gratitude and trust in abundance.

777: Spiritual Awakening and Luck

The number 777 is often associated with divine alignment and spiritual awakening. It signals that you are in sync with the universe, and blessings are on their way.

- **Key Message:** You are on the right path —continue trusting your intuition and embracing your spiritual journey.
- **Spiritual Meaning:** Luck, divine alignment, and spiritual enlightenment.
- **When You See It:** Celebrate your progress and remain open to new insights and opportunities.

Example: Seeing 777 after starting a meditation practice reinforces that you're deepening your spiritual connection.

888: Abundance and Prosperity

The appearance of 888 signifies financial abundance, success, and recognition for your efforts. It's a reminder to keep your energy aligned with prosperity and to trust in the flow of the universe.

- **Key Message:** Embrace the abundance flowing into your life, and continue pursuing your goals with determination.
- **Spiritual Meaning:** Wealth, success, and infinite potential.
- **When You See It:** Focus on gratitude for the blessings already in your life and remain open to receiving more.

Example: Seeing 888 after landing a new job suggests that it's a step toward greater financial stability.

999: Completion and Renewal

The number 999 marks the end of a chapter and the beginning of a new one. It's a call to release what no longer serves you and step into a fresh phase of growth.

- **Key Message:** Let go of the past and embrace new beginnings.
- **Spiritual Meaning:** Completion, renewal, and transformation.
- **When You See It:** Reflect on areas of your life that need closure, and trust that new opportunities are ahead.

Example: Seeing 999 after ending a long-term relationship signals that healing and new possibilities are on the horizon.

Practical Ways to Use Angel Numbers in Manifestation

Acknowledge the Message: When you see an angel number, pause and reflect on what it might be communicating. Use it as an opportunity to check in with your energy and focus.

Incorporate Numbers into Affirmations: Include angel numbers in your daily affirmations or visualization exercises. For example:

- *"I trust the universe to align me with opportunities, as affirmed by the 111 I see."*

Journal Your Observations: Create a dedicated section in your manifestation journal to record the angel numbers you encounter and the insights they bring.

Meditate on Their Meaning: Spend a few minutes meditating on the angel number's significance. Ask yourself:

- *What is this number guiding me to focus on?*
- *How does this message align with my goals?*

Reflecting on the Timing

Angel numbers don't appear randomly—they often show up during moments of significance or decision-making. Reflect on the timing and context of their appearance:

What Were You Thinking? Pay attention to your thoughts when you notice an angel number. Were you contemplating a decision, feeling unsure, or setting an intention?

Example: If you see 222 while debating a choice, it's a sign to trust your intuition and seek balance.

What's Happening in Your Life? Consider how the number relates to your current challenges, goals, or emotions.

Example: If you're starting a new project and see 111, it's a green light from the universe to move forward.

Step-by-Step Angel Number Journaling Practice

Follow these steps to build a consistent and insightful journaling practice:

Record the Angel Number

Each time you notice an angel number, document it in your journal. Include details such as:

- The number you saw (e.g., 222).

- Where and when you saw it (e.g., on a clock at 2:22 PM or on a license plate while driving).
- How you felt at the moment.

Reflect on Your Thoughts and Actions

Write about what you were thinking or doing when the number appeared. This context often holds the key to its meaning. For example:

- Were you contemplating a decision?
- Were you feeling stuck, excited, or uncertain?
- Did the number catch your attention unexpectedly?

Connect the Message to Your Life

Interpret the meaning of the angel number and how it relates to your current situation. Ask yourself:

- *What is this number trying to tell me?*
- *Does it align with a specific goal, challenge, or area of focus in my life?*

Write an Affirmation or Action Step

Based on the number's message, create an affirmation or decide on an action step to align with its guidance. Examples:

- *If you see 444:* Write, "I am supported by the universe and trust in my ability to build a strong foundation."
- *If you see 555:* Commit to embracing a change you've been resisting.

Review and Reflect Regularly

At the end of each week or month, review your journal entries. Look for recurring numbers, patterns, or themes. Reflect on how these messages have guided your decisions and actions.

Prompts for Angel Number Journaling

To deepen your insights, use these prompts when reflecting on angel numbers:

1. What was my immediate reaction to seeing this number?
2. How does this number relate to my current goals or challenges?
3. What emotions arose when I saw the number?
4. What message do I believe the universe is sending me?
5. What action can I take to align with this guidance?

Practical Example of a Journal Entry

Here's a sample journal entry to illustrate the process:

- **Date:** December 28, 2024
- **Number:** 333
- **Where/When:** Saw it on my phone at 3:33 PM while taking a break at work.
- **Thoughts/Feelings:** I was thinking about whether to start a side business. I felt unsure and overwhelmed.
- **Interpretation:** This number reminds me that my spiritual guides are encouraging me to trust my creative instincts and take the first step.
- **Action Step:** Research one small action I can take today to move forward with my idea.
- **Affirmation:** "I am supported by the universe, and I trust in my creative potential."

Trusting Your Intuition with Angel Numbers

Your intuition is your inner compass, a guiding force that connects you to the universe's wisdom. When working with angel numbers, intuition is essential for understanding their unique messages and applying them to your life. This subchapter explores how to strengthen your intuitive abilities, trust your inner guidance, and deepen your connection with angel numbers.

Ask Yourself Questions: When you see an angel number, pause and ask:

- *What am I feeling right now?*
- *What was I thinking about when I noticed this number?*
- *How does this number relate to my current goals or challenges?*

Visualize Your Desired Outcome: Engage in visualization exercises to connect with the energy of your goals. Your intuition will often guide you toward numbers that confirm or refine your vision.

Practice Gratitude: Gratitude raises your vibration and strengthens your connection to the universe, making it easier to trust intuitive insights.

Combining Intuition and Angel Numbers

Your intuition amplifies the power of angel numbers by offering a personalized lens through which to interpret them. Here's how to combine these two tools:

Pause When You See a Number: Take a moment to reflect on what this number might mean for you. *Example:* If you see 777, consider how it relates to your current spiritual journey or recent breakthroughs.

Feel the Emotion of the Moment: Tune into your emotional state when you notice the number. Positive feelings might affirm alignment, while discomfort could suggest the need for recalibration.

Let the Message Guide Your Actions: Use your intuition to decide how to act on the number's guidance. *Example:* If you see 555 and feel a sense of excitement, it might be time to embrace a change you've been avoiding.

Real-Life Stories of Angel Number Guidance

Hearing how others have experienced and interpreted angel numbers can provide valuable insights and inspiration for your own journey. Real-life stories demonstrate the transformative power of these numbers and highlight their ability to provide clarity, reassurance, and direction. In this section, we'll explore several compelling examples of how people have used angel numbers to navigate life's challenges, make decisions, and manifest their desires.

Story 1: Finding Purpose with 111

Case Study: Maya's Career Crossroads

Maya was at a career crossroads, feeling unfulfilled in her corporate job but unsure of what direction to take. She began noticing the number 111 everywhere—on the clock at 1:11, on receipts, and even as a page number in a book she randomly opened.

Her Reflection: Maya realized she was often thinking about her dream of starting her own business when the number appeared. She interpreted 111 as a sign to focus her thoughts on her goal of becoming an entrepreneur.

Her Action: Inspired by the message, Maya started journaling about her vision and creating a step-by-step plan to leave her job.

The Outcome: Within a few months, Maya launched her online business, which quickly gained traction. She credits the repeated appearance of 111 for giving her the confidence to take the leap.

Story 2: Embracing Change with 555

Case Study: David's Move Abroad

David had been considering moving abroad for years but was held back by fear of the unknown. When he began seeing the number 555 on license plates, billboards, and even in his inbox, he felt compelled to investigate its meaning.

His Interpretation: David learned that 555 symbolizes transformation and new opportunities. He took it as a sign that the universe was encouraging him to embrace change.

His Action: With renewed courage, David started the process of applying for jobs overseas.

The Outcome: A few weeks later, he received an offer from a company in his dream city. The move turned out to be one of the best decisions of his life, leading to personal growth and professional success.

Story 3: Rebuilding Relationships with 222

Case Study: Emily's Family Reconnection

Emily had grown distant from her younger brother due to years of misunderstandings. She began seeing 222 frequently, especially during moments of reflection about her family.

Her Reflection: Emily interpreted 222 as a message to bring balance and harmony back into her relationships.

Her Action: She decided to reach out to her brother, initiating a heartfelt conversation that opened the door to reconciliation.

The Outcome: Over time, their relationship improved significantly. Emily now considers 222 her "relationship number" and continues to see it during moments of gratitude for her family.

Story 4: Overcoming Fear with 444

Case Study: Alex's Health Journey

Alex was facing a health challenge that left him feeling anxious and uncertain about the future. During this time, he repeatedly encountered the number 444 —in doctor's offices, on his phone, and even in unexpected places like graffiti.

His Interpretation: Alex discovered that 444 symbolizes protection and support. He felt reassured that he was being guided and cared for by the universe.

His Action: He began incorporating mindfulness practices and affirmations into his daily routine, focusing on the mantra: *"I am protected and supported in my healing journey."*

The Outcome: Alex's mindset shifted from fear to trust, allowing him to approach his treatment with a sense of peace and optimism. He continues to see 444 as a reminder of his inner strength.

Story 5: Manifesting Abundance with 888

Case Study: Sophia's Financial Breakthrough

Sophia had been struggling with finances for years, feeling stuck in a cycle of scarcity. When she started seeing 888, she initially dismissed it as a coincidence but eventually decided to explore its meaning.

Her Reflection: She learned that 888 represents abundance and financial prosperity. Sophia realized she needed to shift her mindset from lack to abundance.

Her Action: She began writing daily affirmations, such as *"I am open to receiving financial blessings."* She also took practical steps to improve her financial situation, like budgeting and seeking new income opportunities.

The Outcome: Within months, Sophia received an unexpected promotion and a freelance opportunity that significantly increased her income. She now sees 888 as a sign of encouragement whenever she needs to refocus on abundance.

Story 6: Letting Go with 999

Case Study: Liam's Fresh Start

Liam was holding onto a toxic relationship, unsure of how to move forward. The number 999 started appearing in his life — on his phone battery percentage, as a random number in conversations, and even in dreams.

His Interpretation: Liam understood that 999 signifies completion and letting go. He realized it was time to release the relationship and make space for new opportunities.

His Action: With this newfound clarity, Liam ended the relationship and focused on self-care and personal growth.

The Outcome: Over time, Liam felt a profound sense of freedom and renewal. He began noticing 111, signaling the start of a new chapter in his life.

Beyond Repeated Numbers: The Full Spectrum of Angel Numbers

Mixed Number Sequences

Angel numbers aren't always about repetition. Sequences like **123, 456, or 789** are just as meaningful and often indicate progress or alignment in your journey.

- **123:** This sequence represents taking things step by step. It's a reminder to trust the process and break your goals into manageable actions.
- **456:** A sign of steady progress, urging you to continue building your life in alignment with your aspirations.
- **789:** Completion of a major cycle, signaling that you're about to transition into something new and exciting.

Mirrored and Reflective Numbers

Mirrored numbers like **121, 343, or 818** hold a message of balance, duality, and introspection. They often encourage you to look within or focus on relationships with others.

- **121:** A call to balance giving and receiving, reminding you that harmony is key to fulfillment.
- **343:** Encouragement to trust in your spiritual guides and believe in the foundations you're building.
- **818:** A powerful signal of new opportunities and abundant potential heading your way.

Palindromic Numbers

Palindromic numbers — those that read the same backward and forward, such as **101, 202, or 303** — symbolize cycles, reflection, and spiritual insight.

- **101:** A reminder to focus on your thoughts as you're laying the groundwork for your reality.
- **202:** Stay centered and trust that balance will guide you through any challenges.
- **303:** Call upon your spiritual support system as you continue growing and evolving.

Dual Sequences

Numbers like **1122, 3344, or 5566** combine the energies of two repeating digits, amplifying their meaning and creating a unique message.

- **1122:** A powerful sign to align with your higher purpose and step confidently into your vision.
- **3344:** Encouragement to keep putting in the effort, knowing that your hard work is supported by universal forces.
- **5566:** A sign that transformative changes are stabilizing into new and exciting opportunities.

Personal and Unique Numbers

Angel numbers can be deeply personal, appearing in sequences that hold unique significance for you. For example:

- **1989:** Your birth year might appear to remind you to reconnect with your authentic self.
- **515:** A specific time or date might catch your attention, signaling an important moment or decision.

Pay attention to how these numbers make you feel, as their significance often relates to personal milestones, memories, or aspirations.

Sequences with Slight Variations

Sometimes, you might notice numbers that aren't perfectly repetitive but still seem to form a pattern, like **1212, 1313, or 1414**. These sequences carry layered meanings:

- **1212:** A call to remain optimistic and trust that new beginnings are unfolding.
- **1313:** Embrace your creative energy and trust in divine support as you pursue your dreams.
- **1414:** Focus on building solid foundations in all areas of your life.

Non-Traditional or Asymmetrical Numbers

Even non-traditional patterns like **321, 747, or 8881** can carry powerful messages, often tied to your current circumstances.

- **321:** Simplify your life and take intentional steps forward.
- **747:** A signal that your spiritual journey is aligning with divine timing.
- **8881:** Reinforces abundance, with an added emphasis on individuality and leadership.

Expand Your Knowledge with a Comprehensive Guide

To help you unlock the full potential of angel numbers, I've created a detailed PDF guide that dives even deeper into their meanings. This guide includes interpretations for hundreds of sequences —beyond just the repetitive patterns — and provides practical tips for recognizing and applying their messages in your daily life.

Scan the QR code at the beginning of this book to download your free PDF:

"The Ultimate Guide to Angel Numbers."

It's your complete resource for decoding the universe's messages and aligning with your highest potential.

Chapter 3: The Law of Attraction Explained

What Is the Law of Attraction?

The Law of Attraction is one of the most intriguing and empowering principles in the realm of personal growth and spirituality. At its core, it states that like attracts like: the energy you project into the universe — through your thoughts, feelings, and actions — ultimately shapes the reality you experience. While this concept may seem simple, its implications are profound, influencing every aspect of life, from relationships and health to career and personal fulfillment.

Understanding the Foundational Principles

The Law of Attraction operates on the premise that everything in the universe, including your thoughts and emotions, is made up of energy vibrating at specific frequencies. When you focus your attention on something, you emit a vibrational signal that attracts experiences, people, and opportunities that resonate with that frequency.

- **Thoughts as Magnets:** Every thought you have carries energy. Positive, empowering thoughts attract circumstances aligned with joy and abundance, while negative, fear-based thoughts can draw challenges or setbacks.
- **The Power of Emotion:** Your emotions amplify your thoughts, acting as a signal booster. Feeling excited, grateful, or hopeful aligns your vibration with what you desire, increasing its likelihood of manifesting.
- **Intentional Focus:** The Law of Attraction doesn't respond to what you want casually — it responds to where you place your consistent focus. By deliberately directing your thoughts toward your goals, you align yourself with their realization.

———

Neuroscience: The Reticular Activating System (RAS)

Your brain is designed to filter information, focusing on what's most relevant to your goals and desires. The Reticular Activating System (RAS), a network of neurons in the brainstem, plays a crucial role in this process.

How the RAS Works: The RAS acts as a gatekeeper for your attention, prioritizing information that aligns with your focus. When you set a clear intention, your RAS helps you notice opportunities, resources, and connections that support your goals.

- *Example:* If you decide to buy a red car, you'll suddenly notice red cars everywhere. This isn't because they've appeared out of nowhere — it's because your RAS is now tuned to spot them.

Reinforcing Your Desires: By repeatedly visualizing and affirming your goals, you program your RAS to prioritize information that aligns with those desires. This creates a feedback loop that supports your manifestation process.

The Psychology of Belief

The Law of Attraction also leverages the power of belief and mindset. Your beliefs shape your thoughts, emotions, and actions, influencing how you interact with the world.

Self-Fulfilling Prophecies: When you believe something is possible, you're more likely to take actions that make it a reality. Conversely, limiting beliefs can create barriers to success.

- *Example:* If you believe you're capable of achieving a promotion, you'll approach opportunities with confidence, increasing your chances of success.

The Placebo Effect: The placebo effect demonstrates how belief can create real, measurable outcomes. In medical studies, patients who believe they're receiving effective treatment often experience improvements, even when given a placebo. This highlights the mind's power to influence physical reality.

Recognizing and Shifting Low-Vibration Patterns

Everyone experiences moments of low-vibration thinking or feeling, but the key to manifestation lies in recognizing these moments and shifting your focus.

Step 1: Awareness: Notice when your thoughts or emotions dip into negativity. Pay attention to your inner dialogue and physical sensations, as these often indicate a shift in energy.

Step 2: Acknowledge Without Judgment: Instead of criticizing yourself, accept that negative thoughts or feelings are natural. Remind yourself that they are temporary and do not define you.

Step 3: Reframe Your Thoughts: Replace low-vibration thoughts with empowering ones. For example:

- Instead of thinking, *"I'm not good enough,"* try, *"I am constantly growing and improving."*

Step 4: Use Emotional Anchors: Engage in activities that raise your vibration, such as listening to uplifting music, practicing gratitude, or visualizing your goals.

Examples of Thought-Vibration Alignment

Manifesting a Dream Job:

- **Thoughts:** "I am excited to find a job that fulfills me."
- **Emotions:** Feel gratitude and excitement as if you already have the job.
- **Outcome:** Opportunities aligned with your vision appear, such as job postings, connections, or interviews.

Attracting a Loving Relationship:

- **Thoughts:** "I am worthy of love and meaningful connections."
- **Emotions:** Feel joy and love as you imagine your ideal partnership.
- **Outcome:** You attract people who resonate with your energy and values.

Creating a Mental and Visual Vision Board

What Is a Vision Board?

A vision board is a collection of images, words, and symbols that represent your goals and desires. By placing these visuals in a space where you can see them regularly, you keep your intentions at the forefront of your mind, reinforcing the vibrational alignment needed to manifest them.

- **Mental Vision Board:** An internal, visualization-based version of a vision board. It involves creating vivid mental images of your goals and the feelings associated with achieving them.
- **Physical Vision Board:** A tangible board crafted with images, text, and objects that symbolize your desires.

Creating a Mental Vision Board

A mental vision board is a portable, flexible tool that allows you to carry your goals and intentions with you wherever you go. Here's how to create one:

Step 1: Define Your Goals.

Start by getting clear about what you want to manifest. Be specific and focus on goals that genuinely excite you. For example:

- Career: "I want a fulfilling job where I earn $10,000 a month."
- Relationships: "I want a loving and supportive partnership."

Step 2: Visualize in Detail

Close your eyes and imagine your goals as if they've already come true. Use all your senses to make the visualization vivid and realistic:

- What do you see?
- What sounds are around you?
- What emotions are you feeling?

Example: If your goal is to move into a dream home, picture the layout, colors, and even the feeling of the carpet under your feet. Imagine yourself celebrating in this home with loved ones.

Step 3: Create an Emotional Connection.

Focus on the emotions associated with achieving your goal. Feel the gratitude, joy, and excitement as if it's already yours. Emotions amplify the vibrational energy of your visualization.

Step 4: Practice Daily.

Set aside a few minutes each day to revisit your mental vision board. Morning and bedtime are particularly effective times, as your mind is more receptive to positive programming during these periods.

Building a Physical Vision Board

A physical vision board adds a tactile dimension to your manifestation practice, making your goals feel even more tangible. Here's how to create one:

Step 1: Gather Your Materials

You'll need:

- A board (corkboard, foam board, or even a large sheet of paper).
- Magazines, printouts, or photos.
- Scissors, glue, or pins.
- Markers or pens for adding text.

Step 2: Select Inspiring Images and Words

Look for visuals that resonate with your goals. These could include:

- Pictures of dream destinations, homes, or experiences.
- Words or quotes that inspire and motivate you.
- Symbols that represent abundance, love, or health.

Step 3: Organize Your Board

Arrange your images and words on the board in a way that feels intuitive and inspiring. You might group similar goals together (e.g., career, relationships, health) or create a collage that represents your overall vision.

Step 4: Place It in a Visible Spot

Position your vision board where you'll see it regularly, such as in your bedroom, office, or meditation space. Frequent exposure reinforces your intentions and keeps you aligned with your goals.

Combining Mental and Physical Vision Boards

While mental and physical vision boards are powerful on their own, using them together can amplify their effects:

Morning Practice: Start your day by visualizing your mental vision board, then spend a few moments looking at your physical board.

Evening Reflection: Before bed, review your physical board and mentally rehearse the feelings and experiences of achieving your goals.

Midday Boost: If you're feeling disconnected or discouraged, take a few moments to visualize your goals or glance at your vision board to reset your focus and energy.

Daily Practices to Strengthen Alignment

Incorporate these practices into your routine to amplify your attraction power:

1. Morning Gratitude Ritual

Start each day with gratitude, setting a positive tone and high vibration for the hours ahead.

How to Do It:

- Write down three things you're grateful for, focusing on both current blessings and what you're manifesting as if it's already yours.
- *Example:* "I am grateful for my supportive family, my vibrant health, and the opportunities that flow effortlessly into my life."

2. Affirmations and Self-Talk

Your inner dialogue shapes your vibration. Positive affirmations rewire your subconscious mind to align with your desires.

How to Use Them:

- Repeat affirmations aloud or silently throughout the day.
- Write them down during your 369 practice for added focus.
- *Examples:*
    - "I am worthy of love and abundance."
    - "Opportunities come to me effortlessly."

3. Visualization Sessions

Take time to vividly imagine your goals as if they've already manifested. This practice bridges the gap between intention and belief.

How to Visualize Effectively:

- Find a quiet space, close your eyes, and picture your desired outcome.
- Engage all your senses: What does it look, sound, smell, or feel like?
- Feel the emotions of joy and gratitude as if it's already real.

Example: If you're manifesting a new home, imagine walking through its rooms, hearing laughter from loved ones, and feeling the comfort of your dream space.

4. Journaling for Manifestation

Journaling is a powerful tool for clarifying your intentions and tracking your progress.

How to Journal:

- Write about your goals in the present tense as if they've already happened.
- Reflect on your emotions, challenges, and any synchronicities you've noticed.
- Use prompts like:

- "What am I manifesting today?"
- "What signs of alignment did I experience this week?"

5. Mindfulness and Meditation

Staying present and centered helps you recognize opportunities and maintain a high vibrational state.

Simple Meditation Practice:

- Sit quietly, focus on your breath, and imagine light or energy filling your body.
- As you exhale, release doubts or fears that no longer serve you.

Mindfulness in Action:

- Pay attention to your surroundings and thoughts throughout the day.
- Redirect negative thoughts with affirmations or gratitude.

6. Inspired Action

Manifestation requires more than visualization—it demands aligned action that brings your desires closer to reality.

How to Identify Inspired Actions:

- Ask yourself: "What step can I take today to move closer to my goal?"
- Trust your intuition to guide you toward opportunities.

Example: If you're manifesting a new career, inspired actions could include networking, updating your resume, or researching potential employers.

Real-Life Stories of Manifestation

Story 1: Manifesting a Dream Job

Case Study: Hannah's Career Breakthrough

Hannah had been working in an unfulfilling job for years, yearning for a position that aligned with her passions and skills. She decided to focus on manifesting her dream role using visualization and affirmations.

Her Process:

- Each morning, she visualized herself thriving in her ideal workplace. She imagined interacting with supportive colleagues, solving creative challenges, and feeling valued.
- She wrote daily affirmations such as, *"I am grateful for my dream job where I feel inspired and successful."*
- She also took inspired action by updating her resume and networking within her industry.

The Outcome: Within two months, Hannah was offered a role at a company she admired, with a salary and work environment exceeding her expectations. She attributes her success to her consistent focus, positive mindset, and proactive steps.

Lesson: Visualization paired with aligned action creates a powerful formula for manifestation.

Story 2: Attracting Financial Abundance

Case Study: Carlos' Financial Transformation

Carlos had always struggled with money and felt stuck in a cycle of scarcity. After learning about the Law of Attraction, he decided to shift his focus from lack to abundance.

His Process:

- Carlos started a gratitude journal, listing things he appreciated about his financial situation, such as having enough to pay bills.
- He visualized himself living a financially abundant life, imagining the freedom and peace it would bring.
- He also took practical steps, such as creating a budget and exploring new income opportunities.

The Outcome: Within six months, Carlos received an unexpected bonus at work, started a successful side business, and cleared his debts. He continued to use the Law of Attraction to build long-term financial stability.

Lesson: Focusing on gratitude and abundance, even in small ways, can shift your financial reality.

Story 3: Manifesting a Loving Relationship

Case Study: Emma's Journey to Love

Emma had been single for years and often felt lonely. She decided to use the Law of Attraction to manifest a meaningful relationship.

Her Process:

- She wrote affirmations such as, *"I am worthy of love and attract a partner who respects and cherishes me."*

- Instead of focusing on the absence of love, Emma started appreciating the relationships she already had, such as those with friends and family.
- She visualized herself in a happy, loving partnership and took inspired action by joining social groups and dating apps with an open, positive attitude.

The Outcome: After several months, Emma met someone who embodied the qualities she had envisioned. They built a strong, loving relationship that continues to thrive.

Lesson: Shifting focus from lack to gratitude and actively participating in opportunities creates space for love to enter your life.

Story 4: Overcoming Health Challenges

Case Study: Alex's Healing Journey

Alex had been struggling with chronic health issues that left him feeling defeated. He decided to use the Law of Attraction to focus on healing and vitality.

His Process:

- Each day, Alex visualized himself feeling energetic and healthy. He imagined himself engaging in activities he loved, free from pain.
- He wrote affirmations like, *"My body is strong, healthy, and resilient."*
- He also adopted healthier habits, such as improving his diet and practicing mindfulness.

The Outcome: Over time, Alex noticed significant improvements in his health. While he still faced challenges, his overall energy and well-being improved dramatically, allowing him to live a more active and fulfilling life.

Lesson: Combining a positive mindset with practical actions creates a holistic approach to healing and wellness.

Story 5: Creating Unexpected Opportunities

Case Study: Priya's Big Move

Priya dreamed of moving to another country but didn't know how to make it happen. She decided to focus her energy on manifesting this goal.

Her Process:

- She visualized herself living in her dream city, imagining the sights, sounds, and experiences.
- She wrote affirmations such as, *"I am so grateful for the exciting new opportunities awaiting me in my new home."*
- She also researched visa requirements, job opportunities, and housing options, preparing for the move.

The Outcome: A few months later, Priya received an unexpected job offer abroad, with relocation assistance included. She made the move and has been thriving ever since.

Lesson: When you align your thoughts and actions, the universe often provides unexpected solutions to achieve your goals.

Chapter 4: The Power of Thought

How Thoughts Shape Reality

The idea that our thoughts can shape our reality might sound abstract, but when viewed through the lenses of neuroscience and spirituality, it becomes a powerful and practical concept. Thoughts are not just fleeting mental constructs; they are energetic signals that influence how we perceive and interact with the world. By understanding how this process works, we can consciously direct our thoughts to create the outcomes we desire.

The Reticular Activating System (RAS): Why Your Brain Filters What You Focus On

The brain processes an overwhelming amount of information every second, but only a small fraction reaches your conscious awareness. The **Reticular Activating System (RAS)**, a network of neurons in your brainstem, acts as a filter, prioritizing what you pay attention to based on your thoughts, beliefs, and goals.

How the RAS Works: The RAS evaluates stimuli and determines what's relevant to you. When you focus on a specific thought or intention, your RAS highlights information that supports it.

- *Example:* If you're thinking about buying a red car, you'll suddenly start noticing red cars everywhere. They didn't magically multiply—you've simply tuned your RAS to filter for them.

Impact on Manifestation: By consciously directing your thoughts toward your desires, you program your RAS to seek opportunities, connections, and resources that align with your goals.

- *Example:* If you set the intention to find a new job, your RAS might make you more aware of job postings, networking events, or conversations that could lead to opportunities.

Practical Examples of How Thought Patterns Influence Outcomes

The influence of thoughts on reality can be seen in everyday examples that highlight the connection between mindset and results.

Career Success: A person who consistently thinks, *"I am valuable and capable of achieving my goals,"* is more likely to notice opportunities for advancement, approach challenges with confidence, and earn the respect of colleagues.

- *Contrast:* Someone who repeatedly thinks, *"I'm not good enough,"* might avoid taking risks, miss opportunities, and reinforce their belief in failure.

Relationships: Focusing on thoughts like, *"I am worthy of love and meaningful connections,"* attracts relationships that reflect those values. On the other hand, thoughts such as, *"No one understands me,"* can create a self-fulfilling prophecy of isolation.

Health and Well-Being: Studies show that people with a positive outlook recover more quickly from illness and maintain better overall health. Thinking, *"My body is strong and capable of healing,"* reinforces behaviors that support well-being, such as exercise and healthy eating.

Financial Abundance: Thoughts of abundance, like, *"I attract wealth effortlessly,"* encourage proactive behaviors, such as budgeting, investing, or seeking new income streams. Conversely, thoughts of scarcity, like, *"I'll never have enough,"* can lead to fear-based decisions that limit growth.

Common Limiting Beliefs About Key Areas of Life

Understanding the types of limiting beliefs can help you pinpoint the ones that may be affecting you:

Money and Abundance:

- *"Money is the root of all evil."*
- *"I'm not smart enough to be wealthy."*

Relationships and Love:

- *"I'll always be alone."*
- *"I'm not lovable or attractive enough."*

Career and Success:

- *"I don't have what it takes to succeed."*
- *"I'm too old (or too young) to achieve my goals."*

Health and Well-Being:

- *"I'm not disciplined enough to be healthy."*
- *"It's too late to make a change."*

Shifting from Limiting to Empowering Beliefs

Once you've identified a limiting belief, you can begin to challenge and rewrite it. Here's how:

Question the Validity of the Belief: Ask yourself:

- *"Is this belief objectively true?"*
- *"What evidence contradicts this belief?"*
    - *Example:* If you believe, *"I'm not good at public speaking,"* reflect on any instances where you communicated effectively.

Reframe the Belief: Transform the limiting belief into a positive, empowering statement.

- **Limiting Belief:** *"I'll never be successful."*
- **Empowering Belief:** *"I have the skills and determination to create my own success."*

Create Supporting Affirmations: Develop affirmations that reinforce your new belief and repeat them daily.

- *"I am capable of achieving my goals."*
- *"I attract opportunities that align with my purpose."*

Take Action to Reinforce the Belief: Action solidifies belief. Start small by taking steps that align with your new mindset.

- *Example:* If you're building confidence in your abilities, volunteer for a project that challenges you.

Rewriting Negative Thought Patterns

Recognize the Thought. The first step to rewriting a negative thought is noticing when it occurs. Awareness is key to breaking the automatic cycle.

What to Watch For:

- Recurring self-doubt, such as "I'm not capable."
- All-or-nothing thinking, like "I always fail."
- Catastrophizing, or expecting the worst-case scenario.

Pause and Reflect: When a negative thought arises, pause and ask yourself:

- *"Is this thought serving me?"*
- *"Would I say this to someone I care about?"*

Challenge the Thought. Negative thoughts often lack factual basis. By questioning their validity, you weaken their hold on your mindset.

Ask Yourself:

- *"What evidence do I have that this thought is true?"*
- *"What evidence contradicts it?"*

Reframe the Narrative:

- Negative Thought: *"I'm terrible at presentations."*
- Reframed Thought: *"I may feel nervous during presentations, but I'm improving with practice."*

Replace with a Positive Thought. Once you've challenged the negative thought, replace it with a positive, empowering one that aligns with your goals.

Examples:

- *"I can't do this"* → *"I am learning and growing every day."*
- *"Nothing ever works out for me"* → *"I trust that everything is unfolding for my highest good."*

Reinforce the New Thought with Action. Taking action that supports your new belief helps solidify it. Small steps build confidence and create momentum.

Example:
If you've replaced *"I'm not capable of success"* with *"I am capable of achieving my goals,"* start by setting and completing a small, achievable task related to your goal.

Techniques for Rewriting Thought Patterns

Daily Affirmations. Affirmations are powerful tools for rewiring your subconscious mind. They counteract negative thoughts and reinforce positive beliefs.

How to Use Them:

- Write down affirmations that resonate with your goals.
- Repeat them aloud or silently throughout the day.
- Pair them with visualization for added impact.

Examples:

- *"I am worthy of love and success."*
- *"I attract opportunities effortlessly."*

Gratitude Practice. Gratitude shifts your focus from lack to abundance, naturally redirecting negative thoughts.

How to Practice:

- Each day, write down three things you're grateful for.
- Reflect on why these things matter to you.
- When a negative thought arises, counter it with gratitude for something positive.

Visualization. Visualization helps you focus on the reality you want to create, replacing negative mental images with positive ones.

How to Visualize:

- Close your eyes and imagine your goal as if it's already achieved.
- Engage all your senses and focus on the emotions it brings.

Example: If you're manifesting confidence, visualize yourself speaking calmly and clearly in a situation that typically makes you nervous.

Journaling. Writing helps clarify your thoughts and identify patterns. Use journaling to explore and reframe negative thoughts.

Prompts to Try:

- *"What limiting belief is holding me back, and why isn't it true?"*
- *"How can I reframe this thought into something empowering?"*

Techniques for Positive Thinking

Start Your Day with Intention. How you begin your day sets the tone for your thoughts and energy. Establish a morning routine that prioritizes positivity.

Morning Affirmations: Begin each day by repeating empowering affirmations that align with your goals.

Examples:

- "I am grateful for this new day filled with opportunities."
- "I attract abundance and joy effortlessly."

Visualization: Spend a few minutes visualizing your ideal day. Imagine yourself navigating challenges with ease and experiencing moments of success and gratitude.

Gratitude Practice: Write down three things you're grateful for before starting your day. This shifts your focus to abundance and primes your mind for positivity.

Practice Mindfulness. Mindfulness is the art of staying present and fully engaged in the moment. It helps you redirect negative thoughts and maintain a calm, positive mindset.

How to Practice Mindfulness:

- Use deep breathing techniques to center yourself during stressful moments.
- Pay attention to your thoughts without judgment, gently guiding them toward positivity.
- Engage fully in daily activities, such as eating or walking, by focusing on the sensations and experiences.

Example: If a negative thought arises, acknowledge it with curiosity, then consciously replace it with a positive affirmation like, *"I choose to focus on solutions, not problems."*

Surround Yourself with Positivity. The people, environments, and media you interact with influence your thoughts and emotions. Surrounding yourself with positive influences reinforces your mindset.

- **Positive Relationships:** Spend time with people who uplift and encourage you. Limit interactions with individuals who drain your energy or perpetuate negativity.
- **Uplifting Content:** Consume books, podcasts, and media that inspire and motivate you. Avoid excessive exposure to negative news or social media that triggers comparison or anxiety.
- **Create a Positive Environment:** Decorate your space with uplifting quotes, images, and colors that boost your mood.

Use the "3-to-1" Rule. For every negative thought or experience, counter it with three positive ones. This simple rule helps rewire your brain to focus on positivity.

Example: If you catch yourself thinking, *"I'll never succeed,"* counter it with three positive affirmations:

- "I am capable of learning and growing."
- "I have succeeded in many ways before."
- "Every day, I get closer to my goals."

Reframe Negative Situations. Reframing involves looking at challenges through a more empowering lens, turning obstacles into opportunities for growth.

How to Reframe:

- Identify the lesson or silver lining in the situation.
- Focus on what you can control, rather than dwelling on what you cannot.
- Ask yourself: *"How can this experience help me grow stronger or wiser?"*

Example: Instead of thinking, *"I failed at this project,"* reframe it as, *"This experience taught me valuable skills I can use next time."*

Anchor Positive Emotions. Anchoring involves associating positive emotions with a physical action or memory, allowing you to access those feelings whenever you need them.

How to Anchor Positivity:

- Think of a moment when you felt truly happy or successful.
- Close your eyes, relive the experience, and focus on the emotions it brings.
- Choose a physical action, like squeezing your thumb and forefinger together, to associate with that feeling.
- Use this anchor whenever you need a boost of positivity.

Take "Positive Action Breaks". Throughout the day, take short breaks to engage in activities that lift your mood and reset your energy.

Ideas for Positive Action Breaks:

- Listen to an uplifting song.
- Take a walk in nature and focus on its beauty.
- Write a quick note of appreciation to someone you care about.

Keep a Positivity Journal. Journaling helps reinforce positive thinking by creating a written record of your progress, gratitude, and intentions.

Daily Prompts:

- "What went well today?"
- "What am I proud of accomplishing?"
- "What's one thing I can look forward to tomorrow?"

Journaling Techniques for Mental Clarity

Stream-of-Consciousness Journaling.

This free-form method involves writing whatever comes to mind without worrying about grammar, structure, or coherence. It's particularly effective for uncovering subconscious thoughts and patterns.

How to Practice:

- Set a timer for 10–15 minutes.
- Write continuously, allowing your thoughts to flow freely.
- Don't censor or judge what you write—simply let it out.

Prompt to Try:

- "What's on my mind right now, and how do I feel about it?"

Gratitude Journaling.

Gratitude journaling shifts your focus to the positive aspects of your life, raising your vibrational frequency and reinforcing an abundance mindset.

How to Practice:

- Each day, write down three things you're grateful for. Be specific and focus on why they matter to you.
- Reflect on moments, people, or experiences that brought you joy.

Prompt to Try:

- *"What am I most grateful for today, and how does it make me feel?"*

Intention Journaling.

Use journaling to clarify your goals and set daily, weekly, or monthly intentions. This technique helps you stay focused and aligned with your desires.

How to Practice:

- Write down your goals as if they've already been achieved.
- Pair each goal with an affirmation or visualization exercise.
- Review your intentions regularly to track progress.

Prompt to Try:

- *"What is my biggest goal right now, and what steps can I take to achieve it?"*

Limiting Belief Journaling.

This method involves identifying and challenging the beliefs that no longer serve you. By rewriting these beliefs, you create space for empowering alternatives.

How to Practice:

- Write down a belief you suspect may be holding you back.
- Reflect on where this belief originated and whether it's objectively true.
- Rewrite the belief into a positive statement.

Prompt to Try:

- *"What belief is stopping me from moving forward, and how can I reframe it into something empowering?"*

Visualization Journaling.

This technique combines visualization and writing to create a vivid mental picture of your desired reality. It reinforces your belief in achieving your goals.

How to Practice:

- Imagine your goal as if it's already accomplished.
- Describe it in detail, including how it looks, feels, and impacts your life.
- Reflect on the emotions associated with achieving this goal.

Prompt to Try:

- *"What does my ideal life look and feel like, and what steps am I taking to create it?"*

Success Journaling.

Documenting your achievements, no matter how small, builds confidence and reinforces a growth mindset.

How to Practice:

- At the end of each day, write down one success or accomplishment.
- Reflect on how this success aligns with your larger goals.

Prompt to Try:

- *"What is one thing I did today that I'm proud of, and how does it bring me closer to my goals?"*

Journaling Prompts for Mental Clarity

If you're not sure where to start, try these prompts to spark reflection and insight:

- *"What do I want most right now, and why does it matter to me?"*
- *"What fear or doubt is holding me back, and how can I overcome it?"*
- *"What is one thing I can let go of to create more space for growth?"*
- *"What signs or synchronicities have I noticed recently, and how do they align with my goals?"*

The Link Between Thoughts and Action

How Thoughts Inspire Action

Thoughts act as the foundation for your actions. They shape your perceptions, influence your decisions, and motivate your behaviors. Here's how this connection works:

Clarifying Your Vision: Positive, focused thoughts help you define your goals with clarity and precision, making it easier to identify the actions needed to achieve them.

- *Example:* Thinking, *"I want to build a successful business,"* leads you to research markets, develop skills, and create a plan.

Building Emotional Energy: Thoughts infused with emotions like excitement, gratitude, and confidence generate energy that propels you toward action.

- *Example:* Visualizing yourself achieving a fitness goal might inspire you to join a gym or start a new workout routine.

Overcoming Resistance: When you focus on empowering thoughts, you're better equipped to push through doubts, fears, or procrastination.

- *Example:* Replacing, *"I'll never be able to do this,"* with, *"Every small step moves me closer to success,"* helps you take action even when progress feels slow.

Aligning Thoughts with Action

For thoughts to lead to meaningful action, they must be aligned with your goals. Misaligned thoughts, such as self-doubt or fear of failure, can sabotage even the best intentions. Here's how to ensure alignment:

Start with Clear Intentions. Before taking action, spend time clarifying your goals. Be specific about what you want to achieve and why it matters.

Prompt to Try:

- *"What is my ultimate goal, and how will achieving it improve my life?"*

Focus on the Outcome, Not the Obstacles. Shift your attention from what could go wrong to what you stand to gain. This mindset fosters confidence and determination.

Example: Instead of thinking, *"What if I fail?"* focus on, *"What will success feel like, and what steps can I take today to move closer to it?"*

Break Goals into Small, Actionable Steps. Large goals can feel overwhelming, but breaking them into smaller, manageable tasks makes progress achievable.

Example: If your goal is to write a book, start with a small step like outlining the first chapter or writing 500 words a day.

Use Visualization to Motivate Action. Visualization bridges the gap between thought and action by helping you mentally rehearse success. This not only builds confidence but also primes your brain to recognize opportunities.

Exercise:
- Spend 5 minutes visualizing yourself completing a specific task and experiencing the satisfaction of accomplishment.
- Imagine the positive impact your actions will have on your life.

The Thought-to-Action Roadmap

Creating a thought-to-action roadmap is a practical way to align your mindset with deliberate steps toward your goals. Here's how to build one:

Step 1: Define Your Goal

Write down a clear, specific goal. *Example:* "I want to launch my online store by June 30."

Step 2: Identify Supporting Thoughts

List positive thoughts and affirmations that support your goal. *Examples:*

- "I am capable of building a successful business."
- "I attract customers who value my products."

Step 3: Break Down the Steps

Divide your goal into smaller, actionable tasks. *Examples for Launching an Online Store:*

- Research platforms.
- Design a logo.
- Upload product listings.
- Promote the store on social media.

Step 4: Schedule and Prioritize

Assign deadlines and priorities to each task to create a timeline for progress. *Example:* Complete research by Week 1, create a logo by Week 2, and launch marketing campaigns by Week 4.

Step 5: Take Consistent Action

Commit to completing at least one task each day. Consistency builds momentum and reinforces your belief in the process. *Example:* Spend 30 minutes daily working on your store, even if it's just brainstorming ideas.

Practical Exercise: Creating a Feedback Loop Tracker

This exercise helps you monitor and refine the relationship between your thoughts and reality:

Step 1: Identify a Current Goal

Write down a specific goal you're working toward.

- *Example:* "I want to improve my confidence in public speaking."

Step 2: Record Your Thoughts

List the thoughts and beliefs you currently hold about this goal.

- **Positive:** *"I enjoy sharing ideas with others."*
- **Negative:** *"I always mess up in front of a crowd."*

Step 3: Take Aligned Action

Choose an action that aligns with your positive thoughts.

- *Example:* Practice delivering a short speech in front of friends to build confidence.

Step 4: Reflect on the Outcome

After taking action, write down what happened and how it made you feel.

- *Example:* "I felt nervous but received encouraging feedback. I'm improving."

Step 5: Refine Your Thoughts

Based on the outcome, refine your thoughts to reinforce positivity.

- *Example:* Replace, *"I always mess up,"* with, *"Every time I practice, I get better."*

Chapter 5: The 7-Day Manifestation Routine

The **7-Day Manifestation Routine** is a focused, intentional process designed to help you align your thoughts, energy, and actions with your deepest desires. This framework integrates the principles of Project 369, the Law of Attraction, and the symbolism of angel numbers, all within the transformative power of a seven-day cycle. Each day is crafted to guide you through clear steps that reprogram your mindset, elevate your vibration, and initiate the changes you want to see in your life.

Day 1: Clarity of Desire

The first day of your 7-day manifestation routine is all about setting a clear and focused intention. Clarity is the cornerstone of manifestation—when you know exactly what you want and why you want it, you send a powerful signal to the universe. This signal becomes the foundation for aligning your thoughts, emotions, and actions with your goal.

The Power of Clarity

When your desires are vague, your energy is scattered, and it becomes difficult to attract meaningful results. Clarity not only strengthens your manifestation efforts but also helps you identify the steps needed to achieve your goals.

Why It Matters:

- Clarity reduces confusion and doubt, both of which lower your vibrational energy.
- It sharpens your focus, allowing you to direct your thoughts and actions toward a specific outcome.
- It builds confidence in your ability to manifest.

Questions to Reflect On:

- What do I want to manifest, and why is this important to me?
- How will achieving this goal improve my life or the lives of others?
- What emotions do I associate with achieving this desire?

Morning Ritual: Define Your Desire

Begin your day by defining your primary goal with precision and intention.

Write Your Desire (3 Times):

- Use clear, positive, and present-tense language.
- Example: *"I am grateful to earn $10,000 a month doing work I love."*
- Tip: Focus on the essence of your desire, rather than how it will manifest. Trust the universe to handle the details.

Visualize Your Goal:

- Spend 2–3 minutes imagining your life with this goal already achieved.
- Engage all your senses: What do you see, hear, or feel?
- Example: If you're manifesting financial abundance, visualize yourself paying bills with ease, enjoying a vacation, or investing in your dreams.

Set a Daily Intention:

- Write down one action you can take today to align with your goal.
- Example: *"Today, I will research freelance opportunities that align with my skills."*

Afternoon Focus: Reinforce Your Desire

Revisit your goal in the middle of the day to maintain alignment and build momentum.

Write Your Desire (6 Times):

- Expand on your morning affirmation by including an emotional component.
- Example: *"I feel grateful and fulfilled as I earn $10,000 a month doing work I love."*

Mindfulness Practice:

- Take a 5-minute mindfulness break to reconnect with your goal.
- Close your eyes, breathe deeply, and repeat your affirmation silently.

Inspired Action:

- Take one small step toward your goal, no matter how simple.
- Example: Reach out to a mentor, research tools for your project, or organize your workspace.

Evening Reflection: Solidify Your Focus

End your day by reaffirming your goal and reflecting on your progress.

Write Your Desire (9 Times):

- Repeat your affirmation, feeling the emotions of already achieving your goal.
- Example: *"I am so grateful and excited to earn $10,000 a month doing work I love."*

Reflect on the Day:

- Write down one thing you did today that aligned with your goal.

- Example: *"I reached out to a potential client and felt confident about my skills."*

Visualize Before Sleep:

- Spend 5–10 minutes visualizing your desire. Imagine the details vividly and feel the emotions associated with achieving it.
- This primes your subconscious mind to work on your goal while you sleep.

Additional Exercises for Day 1

If you have extra time, try these exercises to deepen your clarity and connection to your goal:

Journal About Your Desire:

- Write a paragraph or two about why this goal is important to you and how it aligns with your values.

Create a Mind Map:

- Use a mind map to explore the steps and resources needed to achieve your goal. This helps you break it into actionable tasks.

Affirmation Refinement:

- Experiment with different affirmations until you find one that resonates deeply with you.

Key Takeaways for Day 1

- Clarity is the foundation of manifestation. Take time to define your desire in detail and focus on the emotions it evokes.
- Writing your affirmation 3, 6, and 9 times throughout the day helps solidify your intention and keeps it top of mind.

- Visualization and inspired action work together to align your thoughts, emotions, and behaviors with your goal.

Day 2: Gratitude and Abundance

Gratitude is a powerful practice that shifts your focus from what you lack to what you already have. By cultivating an attitude of gratitude, you raise your vibration and align yourself with the energy of abundance. On Day 2 of the 7-Day Manifestation Routine, we'll focus on using gratitude to amplify your manifestation efforts.

The Power of Gratitude in Manifestation

Gratitude is more than just a positive feeling—it's a transformational practice that rewires your brain, elevates your mood, and strengthens your connection with the universe.

Why Gratitude Works:

- **Shifts Your Perspective:** Gratitude helps you focus on abundance rather than scarcity, creating a mindset of positivity.
- **Raises Your Vibration:** When you feel thankful, you emit high-frequency energy, which attracts more high-vibration experiences.
- **Strengthens Neural Pathways:** Practicing gratitude consistently reinforces pathways in your brain that default to optimism and contentment.

Morning Ritual: Gratitude and Intention

Start your day by combining your desire with a sense of thankfulness.

Write Your Desire (3 Times) with Gratitude:

- Add an element of gratitude to your affirmation.
- Example: *"I am grateful to earn $10,000 a month doing work I love, and I appreciate the opportunities that make it possible."*

Gratitude Practice:

- List three things you're grateful for in your current life.
- Be specific and focus on the feelings these blessings evoke.
- Example: *"I'm grateful for the delicious breakfast I enjoyed, the supportive conversation I had with a friend, and the sunny weather."*

Set a Daily Gratitude Intention:

- Write down one way you can express gratitude today.
- Example: *"Today, I will thank a colleague for their help on a recent project."*

Afternoon Focus: Expanding Gratitude

Revisit your desire and explore the abundance you already have.

Write Your Desire (6 Times):

- Use gratitude to connect your current blessings with your future goal.
- Example: *"I am deeply grateful for the financial security I have now and the $10,000 a month I am manifesting."*

Mindful Gratitude Exercise:

- Take 5–10 minutes to focus on the abundance around you. This could be the beauty of nature, the comfort of your home, or the kindness of others.
- As you notice each thing, silently say, *"Thank you."*

Take an Inspired Action with Gratitude:

- Do something meaningful to express gratitude, such as writing a thank-you note, donating to a cause, or helping someone in need.

Evening Reflection: Gratitude and Visualization

End your day by reinforcing gratitude and aligning with your desire.

Write Your Desire (9 Times):

- Feel a deep sense of gratitude as you write, imagining that your goal has already been achieved.
- Example: *"I am so grateful and fulfilled to earn $10,000 a month doing work I love."*

Reflect on Your Gratitude Wins:

- Write down three moments from the day that brought you joy or appreciation.
- Example: *"I'm grateful for the warm smile of a stranger, the productive meeting at work, and the relaxing walk I took in the evening."*

Visualize Your Goal with Gratitude:

- Spend 5–10 minutes visualizing your desired outcome, focusing on how thankful you feel for its manifestation.

Additional Exercises for Day 2

If you want to deepen your gratitude practice, try these activities:

Create a Gratitude Jar:

- Write down one thing you're grateful for each day and place it in a jar. At the end of the week or month, review your notes to reflect on your blessings.

Gratitude Walk:

- Take a walk outdoors and notice everything you appreciate—the fresh air, the trees, or the sound of birds. Say "thank you" for each thing you observe.

Write a Gratitude Letter:

- Write a letter to someone who has positively impacted your life, expressing your appreciation for their kindness, support, or inspiration.

Key Takeaways for Day 2

- Gratitude shifts your focus from lack to abundance, raising your vibration and amplifying your manifestation efforts.
- Combining your desire with gratitude strengthens your emotional connection to your goal.
- Daily practices like gratitude journaling, reflection, and inspired action reinforce a mindset of abundance.

Day 3: Releasing Limiting Beliefs

Day 3 of the 7-Day Manifestation Routine focuses on identifying and releasing limiting beliefs that may be blocking your ability to manifest. These subconscious patterns often go unnoticed but can significantly impact your thoughts, actions, and vibrational energy. By addressing them, you create space for empowering beliefs that align with your goals.

The Role of Limiting Beliefs in Manifestation

Limiting beliefs act like filters, shaping how you perceive the world and what you believe is possible. They often stem from past experiences, cultural conditioning, or fear of failure.

Why Releasing Them Matters:

- Limiting beliefs create resistance, lowering your vibration and misaligning your energy with your desires.
- They can lead to self-sabotage, procrastination, or avoidance of opportunities.
- Replacing them with empowering beliefs removes barriers and strengthens your manifestation process.

Morning Ritual: Identify Your Limiting Beliefs

Begin your day by reflecting on the thoughts and beliefs that may be hindering your progress.

Write Your Desire (3 Times):

- State your goal clearly and confidently.
- Example: *"I am grateful to earn $10,000 a month doing work I love."*

Reflect on Resistance:

- Spend 5 minutes journaling about any doubts or fears that arise when you think about your goal.
- Prompt: *"What thoughts or feelings make me hesitate when I imagine achieving this goal?"*
- Example: *"I feel like success is hard to achieve, or I don't deserve this level of abundance."*

Set an Intention to Release:

- Write a statement affirming your willingness to let go of limiting beliefs.
- Example: *"Today, I release any belief that no longer serves me and replace it with thoughts of abundance."*

Afternoon Focus: Rewrite Limiting Beliefs

Midday is a powerful time to reframe negative thoughts into empowering ones.

Write Your Desire (6 Times):

- Reinforce your goal by pairing it with a positive affirmation.
- Example: *"I am deeply grateful to earn $10,000 a month because I am capable and deserving of success."*

Identify and Reframe a Limiting Belief:

- Choose one belief that surfaced during your morning reflection. Write it down, then reframe it into a positive, empowering statement.
- Example:
    - Limiting Belief: *"I'm not experienced enough to earn this much."*
    - Empowering Belief: *"I am constantly learning and growing, and my experience is valuable."*

Take an Inspired Action:

- Act in alignment with your new belief to reinforce it.
- Example: If you've reframed a belief about your skills, spend 30 minutes learning something new or applying your knowledge.

Evening Reflection: Solidify New Beliefs

End your day by affirming your progress and anchoring your new mindset.

Write Your Desire (9 Times):

- Write it with conviction and include the empowering belief you created earlier.

- Example: *"I am so grateful to earn $10,000 a month because I am skilled, deserving, and capable."*

Reflect on the Day:

- Journal about how it felt to challenge and rewrite a limiting belief.
- Prompt: *"How did rewriting this belief change the way I see myself and my goal?"*

Visualize with Empowered Confidence:

- Spend 5–10 minutes imagining your life with your goal achieved, focusing on how your new belief supports this vision.

Additional Exercises for Day 3

If you want to deepen your practice, try these exercises:

Belief Inventory:

- Make a list of all the beliefs you hold about your goal. Mark the ones that feel limiting and work on reframing them over the next week.

Meditation for Releasing Resistance:

- Use a guided meditation to release fear and self-doubt. Visualize your limiting beliefs dissolving and being replaced with empowering ones.

Affirmation Wall:

- Write your new, positive beliefs on sticky notes and place them where you'll see them daily, such as your mirror or workspace.

Key Takeaways for Day 3

- Identifying and releasing limiting beliefs clears the way for positive, empowering thoughts that align with your desires.
- Reframing these beliefs into supportive affirmations strengthens your mindset and raises your vibration.
- Taking inspired action helps solidify your new beliefs and reinforces your confidence.

Day 4: Emotional Resonance

On Day 4 of the 7-Day Manifestation Routine, we focus on the power of emotions in the manifestation process. Emotions act as a bridge between your thoughts and the energy you send out into the universe. By cultivating emotions that resonate with your desires, you align your vibration with the reality you wish to attract.

Why Emotional Resonance Matters

Manifestation is not just about thinking your way to success—it's about feeling your way there. When your emotions match the frequency of your desires, you amplify your ability to manifest.

- **Emotions Amplify Energy:** Positive emotions like joy, gratitude, and excitement strengthen the vibration of your intentions.
- **Feelings Signal Alignment:** The emotions you experience act as a compass, showing whether you're aligned with abundance or resistance.
- **Manifestation Begins with Feeling:** The universe responds to your vibrational state, which is shaped by your dominant emotions.

Morning Ritual: Feel Into Your Desire

Start the day by creating an emotional connection to your goal.

Write Your Desire (3 Times):

- Add an emotional component to your affirmation.
- Example: *"I am so grateful and excited to earn $10,000 a month doing work I love."*

Emotional Visualization:

- Spend 5 minutes imagining your goal as if it's already achieved. Focus on the emotions it brings.
- Example: If your goal is financial abundance, feel the freedom, security, and joy it provides.

Set an Emotional Intention:

- Write down an emotion you want to embody throughout the day.
- Example: *"Today, I choose to feel abundant and joyful."*

Afternoon Focus: Strengthen Emotional Alignment

Revisit your goal and deepen your emotional connection.

Write Your Desire (6 Times):

- Focus on the emotions you feel as you write.
- Example: *"I feel deeply fulfilled and grateful to earn $10,000 a month doing work I love."*

Anchor Positive Emotions:

- Recall a time when you felt the emotion you want to embody (e.g., joy, confidence, or gratitude).

- Associate this feeling with a physical gesture, like squeezing your thumb and forefinger together. Use this gesture to anchor the emotion whenever you need it.

Take an Inspired Action with Feeling:

- Choose an action that makes you feel closer to your goal.
- Example: Treat yourself to a small indulgence that reflects the abundance you're manifesting, such as a fancy coffee or a new journal.

Evening Reflection: Reinforce Emotional Resonance

End your day by celebrating the emotions you cultivated.

Write Your Desire (9 Times):

- Write it with deep emotional engagement, imagining the fulfillment of your goal.
- Example: *"I am overflowing with gratitude and excitement as I earn $10,000 a month doing work I love."*

Reflect on Your Emotional Wins:

- Journal about how you felt throughout the day and any moments where you experienced alignment with your goal.
- Prompt: *"What emotions did I embody today, and how did they bring me closer to my desires?"*

Emotional Visualization Before Sleep:

- Spend 5–10 minutes visualizing your goal and immersing yourself in the emotions of having already achieved it.

Additional Exercises for Day 4

Deepen your emotional resonance with these optional exercises:

Create an Emotion Board:

- Similar to a vision board, but focused on the emotions you want to experience. Include images, colors, or words that evoke those feelings.

Gratitude Amplifier:

- Write a gratitude letter to yourself as if your goal has already been achieved.
- Example: *"Thank you for working so hard and manifesting the career of your dreams. You deserve this abundance!"*

Music for Manifestation:

- Listen to music that evokes the emotions you want to feel. Let the rhythm and lyrics deepen your emotional connection to your goal.

Key Takeaways for Day 4

- Emotional resonance is the key to aligning your vibration with your desires.
- Visualizing your goal with positive emotions strengthens your connection to it.
- Cultivating high-vibration emotions throughout the day keeps you aligned with abundance and joy.

Day 5: Inspired Action

Day 5 is all about turning your thoughts and emotions into deliberate actions. While visualization and emotional resonance set the foundation for manifestation, taking inspired action bridges the gap between intention and reality. By aligning your actions with your desires, you create momentum and invite opportunities into your life.

What Is Inspired Action?

Inspired action is different from ordinary action. It's intentional, aligned with your goals, and often feels intuitive or motivated by a sense of excitement or purpose.

Why Inspired Action Matters:

- **Signals Commitment:** Taking action shows the universe you're serious about your goal.
- **Creates Opportunities:** Action sets events in motion, leading to synchronicities and unexpected breakthroughs.
- **Strengthens Belief:** Completing small, aligned tasks reinforces your confidence and belief in your ability to manifest.

How to Recognize Inspired Action:

- It feels natural or exciting rather than forced.
- It aligns with your intuition or a gut feeling.
- It directly supports the realization of your desire.

Morning Ritual: Set the Stage for Action

Start your day with clarity and a focus on taking meaningful steps.

Write Your Desire (3 Times):

- Reinforce your goal and include an action-oriented affirmation.

- Example: *"I am grateful to earn $10,000 a month doing work I love, and I take inspired steps toward this every day."*

Identify One Action for the Day:

- Reflect on a small but meaningful step you can take to support your goal.
- Example: *"Today, I will research three new clients to pitch my services to."*

Visualize Success:

- Spend 2–3 minutes imagining yourself completing this action and the positive outcomes it creates.
- Example: Visualize sending emails to potential clients and receiving enthusiastic responses.

Afternoon Focus: Take Inspired Action

The afternoon is the time to put your plans into motion.

Write Your Desire (6 Times):

- Write it with a focus on the actions you're taking and the results they're creating.
- Example: *"I am deeply grateful to earn $10,000 a month doing work I love, and I attract opportunities through my actions."*

Complete Your Inspired Action:

- Carry out the task you identified in the morning.
- Focus on the positive energy and purpose behind the action rather than the outcome.

Reflect on the Experience:

- Journal for a few minutes about how it felt to take action and any results or insights you noticed.

- Prompt: *"What did I learn or accomplish by taking this step today?"*

Evening Reflection: Celebrate and Plan

End your day by acknowledging your progress and setting the stage for continued action.

Write Your Desire (9 Times):

- Include gratitude for the actions you took and the results they are generating.
- Example: *"I am so grateful and excited to earn $10,000 a month doing work I love, and I celebrate every step I take toward this goal."*

Celebrate Small Wins:

- Reflect on one thing you accomplished today, no matter how small, and celebrate it as a step forward.
- Example: *"I reached out to a new client and felt confident about presenting my ideas."*

Plan for Tomorrow:

- Write down one action you'll take the next day to maintain momentum.
- Example: *"Tomorrow, I will refine my pitch and follow up with a potential client."*

Additional Exercises for Day 5

If you have extra time, try these activities to amplify the impact of your inspired actions:

Create an Action Plan:

- Break your goal into smaller, actionable steps. Write a timeline for completing them over the next week or month.

Mind Map Your Goal:

- Visualize all the actions, resources, and opportunities connected to your desire. Use a mind map to explore how they interrelate.

Accountability Partner:

- Share your action plan with a trusted friend or mentor who can encourage you and provide feedback.

Tips for Maintaining Momentum

- **Stay Flexible:** Inspired actions may not always go as planned. Be open to adjusting your approach based on new insights or opportunities.
- **Focus on Progress, Not Perfection:** Even small steps move you closer to your goal. Celebrate the effort, not just the result.
- **Trust the Process:** Some actions may not yield immediate results, but they contribute to the larger picture. Trust that each step has a purpose.

Key Takeaways for Day 5

- Inspired action is the bridge between thought and reality. By taking deliberate, aligned steps, you create momentum and invite opportunities.
- Celebrate progress, reflect on your actions, and plan your next steps to maintain alignment with your goal.
- Trust your intuition and follow the actions that feel natural, purposeful, and exciting.

Day 6: Synchronicities and Signs

Day 6 focuses on recognizing and interpreting the guidance and confirmations the universe sends through synchronicities and signs. These meaningful coincidences and symbolic messages, such as angel numbers, help you stay aligned with your manifestation journey, providing reassurance and direction.

What Are Synchronicities and Signs?

Synchronicities are events or occurrences that seem too significant to be mere coincidence. Signs often manifest as patterns, symbols, or messages that resonate with your thoughts, desires, or goals.

Why They Matter:

- **Confirmation:** They validate that you're on the right path, reinforcing your belief in the manifestation process.
- **Guidance:** Synchronicities provide subtle hints or nudges to take specific actions or adjust your approach.
- **Connection:** Recognizing signs strengthens your awareness of the universe's support and alignment with your energy.

How to Recognize Synchronicities

Synchronicities and signs can appear in various forms, including:

- **Angel Numbers:** Repeating sequences like 111, 222, or 333 that carry specific vibrational meanings.
- **Meaningful Conversations:** Overhearing words or phrases that align with your current thoughts or goals.
- **Objects or Symbols:** Seeing a recurring image, such as a feather, butterfly, or particular color, that feels significant.
- **Unexpected Opportunities:** A chance meeting or event that seems perfectly timed to support your goals.

Morning Ritual: Set an Intention to Notice Signs

Start your day by opening yourself to guidance from the universe.

Write Your Desire (3 Times):

- Include a request for clarity or confirmation.
- Example: *"I am grateful to earn $10,000 a month doing work I love. I welcome the universe's guidance and signs."*

Set a Mindful Intention:

- Write an affirmation to remain present and aware throughout the day.
- Example: *"Today, I am open to noticing synchronicities and interpreting the signs that guide me."*

Visualize Receiving Signs:

- Spend 2–3 minutes imagining yourself noticing and understanding meaningful messages from the universe.

Afternoon Focus: Be Present and Observant

Throughout the day, stay mindful of your surroundings and the signs that may appear.

Write Your Desire (6 Times):

- Focus on gratitude and openness to synchronicities.
- Example: *"I am deeply grateful to earn $10,000 a month and for the signs that guide me toward this goal."*

Mindfulness Practice:

- Take a 5-minute break to center yourself and observe your environment.
- Ask: *"What patterns, symbols, or messages am I noticing today?"*

Document Synchronicities:

- Keep a journal or notes app handy to record any meaningful signs or occurrences you encounter.
- Example: "I saw 111 three times today, which reminded me to focus on my intentions."

Evening Reflection: Interpret and Appreciate Signs

End your day by reflecting on the synchronicities you noticed and their potential meanings.

Write Your Desire (9 Times):

- Reinforce your gratitude for both your goal and the guidance you received.
- Example: *"I am so grateful to earn $10,000 a month doing work I love, and for the signs that align me with this goal."*

Reflect on Synchronicities:

- Write about the signs you observed and what they mean to you.
- Prompt: *"What synchronicities or signs did I notice today, and how do they confirm or guide my journey?"*

Gratitude Visualization:

- Spend 5–10 minutes visualizing your goal while thanking the universe for its guidance and support.

Understanding Angel Numbers

Angel numbers are a powerful form of synchronicity. Each sequence carries a unique vibrational meaning that aligns with your intentions.

Examples of Angel Numbers and Their Meanings:

- **111:** New beginnings, focus on your intentions.
- **222:** Trust the process and maintain balance.
- **333:** Alignment with mind, body, and spirit; encouragement from the universe.
- **444:** Foundation and stability, reminding you to stay grounded.
- **555:** Major changes or transformations are on the horizon.
- **777:** Spiritual growth and alignment with divine wisdom.

How to Respond to Angel Numbers:

- Pause and reflect on your current thoughts or actions when you see them.
- Consider their meanings in relation to your goals.

Additional Exercises for Day 6

If you want to dive deeper into understanding and leveraging synchronicities, try these activities:

Create a Signs Journal:

- Dedicate a notebook to recording synchronicities, angel numbers, and meaningful coincidences. Reflect on patterns over time.

Meditation for Clarity:

- Spend 10–15 minutes in meditation, focusing on openness to universal guidance. Visualize yourself noticing and interpreting signs effortlessly.

Research Angel Numbers:

- Spend time learning about the meanings of different angel numbers and how they apply to your current goals.

Key Takeaways for Day 6

- Synchronicities and signs are the universe's way of providing guidance and confirmation.
- Staying present and observant helps you notice and interpret these messages.
- Recognizing and appreciating signs strengthens your alignment with your desires and builds trust in the manifestation process.

Day 7: Trust and Surrender

The final day of the 7-Day Manifestation Routine is about letting go of attachment to your goal and placing your trust in the process. Trust and surrender are critical components of manifestation, as they signal your confidence in the universe's ability to align events in your favor. By releasing resistance and focusing on gratitude, you create space for your desires to flow into your life naturally.

Why Trust and Surrender Matter

- **Trust Eliminates Doubt:** Faith in the process removes mental and emotional blocks that can delay manifestation.
- **Surrender Signals Confidence:** Letting go of the "how" and "when" shows that you believe your desires are already on their way.
- **Divine Timing:** The universe often delivers results in unexpected ways or at the perfect moment, even if it's not the timeline you initially envisioned.

Morning Ritual: Trust the Process

Start your final day with affirmations and gratitude, focusing on trust and surrender.

Write Your Desire (3 Times):

- Reinforce your goal with a focus on trust.
- Example: *"I am grateful to earn $10,000 a month doing work I love, and I trust the universe to bring this to me in perfect timing."*

Affirmation of Trust:

- Write or repeat a statement that emphasizes your confidence in the process.
- Example: *"Everything is unfolding for my highest good, and I release the need to control the outcome."*

Gratitude Meditation:

- Spend 5 minutes meditating on gratitude for all that you have and all that is coming. Feel the joy and peace of knowing your desires are already yours.

Afternoon Focus: Practice Surrender

Dedicate the middle of the day to releasing attachment and finding joy in the present moment.

Write Your Desire (6 Times):

- Emphasize the peace and trust you feel about your goal.
- Example: *"I am deeply grateful to earn $10,000 a month doing work I love, and I release all resistance as it flows to me."*

Mindful Letting Go Exercise:

- Write down any fears, doubts, or worries you still hold about your goal.
- Imagine placing them in a balloon and letting it float away. Visualize yourself feeling lighter and more at ease.

Find Joy in the Present:

- Engage in an activity that brings you happiness, such as spending time with loved ones, enjoying a hobby, or taking a walk in nature. Focusing on joy shifts your energy to abundance.

Evening Reflection: Celebrate and Release

Conclude your week of manifestation with a sense of completion and confidence.

Write Your Desire (9 Times):

- Include gratitude and a statement of surrender.
- Example: *"I am so grateful and excited to earn $10,000 a month doing work I love. I trust the universe to deliver this to me in divine timing."*

Reflect on the Week:

- Journal about the progress you've made, the synchronicities you've noticed, and how your mindset has shifted.
- Prompt: *"How has my understanding of manifestation deepened over the past seven days?"*

Visualize with Gratitude and Trust:

- Spend 5–10 minutes visualizing your goal. This time, focus on the feeling of already having it while releasing all attachment to the outcome.

Additional Exercises for Day 7

If you want to solidify your trust and surrender practice, try these activities:

Create a "Letting Go" Ritual:

- Write down your goal on a piece of paper. As you burn, bury, or release it, say: *"I trust the universe to fulfill this desire in the best possible way."*

Focus on Divine Timing:

- Write an affirmation about trusting the timing of your manifestation.
- Example: *"Everything I desire comes to me at the perfect moment for my growth and joy."*

Gratitude for the Journey:

- Write a thank-you letter to the universe for the experiences, insights, and progress you've gained during this 7-day practice.

Key Takeaways for Day 7

- Trust and surrender are essential for allowing the universe to work in harmony with your intentions.
- Letting go of control and focusing on joy opens the flow of abundance.
- Celebrate your progress and have faith that your desires are on their way, even if the results aren't immediately visible.

Completing the 7-Day Manifestation Routine

Congratulations on completing the 7-Day Manifestation Routine! Over the past week, you've built a strong foundation for aligning your thoughts, emotions, and actions with your goals. While this marks the end of this focused practice, the principles you've learned can be integrated into your daily life for ongoing manifestation success.

Next Steps: Sustaining Your Manifestation Practice

1. **Repeat the Routine:** Revisit the 7-day framework whenever you want to refocus on a specific goal.
2. **Incorporate Key Practices:** Continue gratitude journaling, visualization, and inspired action as part of your daily routine.
3. **Celebrate Progress:** Regularly reflect on the signs, synchronicities, and results you've experienced.
4. **Trust the Process:** Manifestation is an ongoing journey. Trust that the universe is always working in your favor.

Chapter 8: Expanding Your Manifestation Power

Advanced Techniques: Guided Meditation, Detailed Scripting, and Emotional Anchoring

As you deepen your manifestation practice, advanced techniques can amplify your power to align thoughts, emotions, and actions with your desires. Guided meditation, detailed scripting, and emotional anchoring are transformative tools that enhance your connection to your goals and help you sustain a high vibrational frequency.

Guided Meditation for Manifestation

Guided meditation helps quiet the mind, center your energy, and immerse you in the feeling of already having what you desire. It's a powerful way to focus your intention and raise your vibration.

Why It Works

- Calms the mind and reduces resistance by shifting you into a relaxed, receptive state.
- Helps you visualize your goals vividly, creating a strong emotional connection.
- Reinforces your alignment with the universe and the energy of abundance.

How to Practice Guided Meditation
Set the Scene:

- Choose a quiet, comfortable space where you won't be interrupted.
- Use candles, soft lighting, or soothing music to create a relaxing atmosphere.

Prepare Your Mind:

- Sit or lie down in a comfortable position.
- Close your eyes and take a few deep breaths, inhaling for four counts, holding for four counts, and exhaling for four counts.

Visualize Your Desire:

- Imagine your goal as vividly as possible.
- Engage all your senses: See the details, hear the sounds, feel the textures, and even smell or taste aspects of your desired reality.
- Example: If you're manifesting a dream home, visualize walking through its rooms, hearing laughter in the kitchen, and feeling the warmth of the sun streaming through the windows.

Add Emotion:

- Focus on the feelings associated with achieving your goal: joy, gratitude, excitement, or peace.
- Let these emotions fill your entire being.

End with Gratitude:

- Conclude the meditation by thanking the universe for aligning you with your desires.

Pro Tip: Use guided meditation apps or pre-recorded scripts that align with your goals. These can help you stay focused and deepen your practice.

Detailed Scripting

Scripting is a creative and immersive manifestation technique where you write about your goals as if they've already happened. It combines visualization with written affirmations to solidify your intentions and bring them to life.

Why It Works

- Activates your imagination and helps you clarify your desires.
- Creates a sense of certainty by anchoring your goals in the present tense.
- Engages your emotions, which amplify your vibrational energy.

How to Practice Scripting

Set the Scene:

- Choose a quiet time and space where you can focus.
- Use a journal or notebook that's dedicated to your scripting practice.

Write in the Present Tense:

- Describe your desired reality as if it's already happening. Use detailed, vivid language to make it feel real.
- Example:
    - Instead of: *"I want a successful business,"* write: *"I am the proud owner of a thriving business that brings me joy and financial abundance every day."*

Engage Your Senses and Emotions:

- Include sensory details and emotional elements.
- Example: *"As I sit at my desk in my sunlit office, I feel immense gratitude for the creative projects I'm working on. The sound of my keyboard fills me with excitement as I watch my ideas come to life."*

Focus on Gratitude:

- End your script with a note of thanks to the universe for manifesting your desires.
- Example: *"Thank you, universe, for aligning everything perfectly and bringing this beautiful life to me."*

Revisit and Reflect:

- Read your script daily to reinforce your connection to your goals. Let the emotions of your written words inspire you each time.

Pro Tip: Combine scripting with your 369 practice by writing affirmations that align with your script. This reinforces your focus and emotional alignment.

Emotional Anchoring

Emotional anchoring is the practice of associating positive emotions with specific actions, gestures, or triggers, making it easier to access those emotions when you need them most. This technique helps you sustain high-vibration feelings throughout your day.

Why It Works

- Reinforces positive emotions and connects them to your intentions.
- Helps you shift quickly from low to high-vibration states.
- Strengthens the emotional resonance needed for manifestation.

How to Practice Emotional Anchoring

Identify a Positive Emotion:

- Choose an emotion that aligns with your goal, such as joy, confidence, gratitude, or peace.

Recall a Powerful Memory:

- Think of a moment when you felt that emotion strongly.
- Example: If you're anchoring gratitude, recall a time when you received unexpected kindness or achieved something meaningful.

Create a Physical Anchor:

- Associate the emotion with a physical gesture, such as squeezing your thumb and forefinger together, touching your heart, or pressing your palms together.

Reinforce the Anchor:

- While recalling the memory and feeling the emotion, perform the gesture repeatedly.
- Visualize your goal and let the positive emotion grow stronger each time you perform the anchor.

Use the Anchor Daily:

- Whenever you feel doubt or resistance, use your physical anchor to instantly shift into the desired emotional state.

Pro Tip: Pair emotional anchoring with affirmations or visualization to enhance its effect. For example, as you visualize your goal, use the anchor gesture to intensify your emotions.

Combining These Techniques

To maximize your manifestation power, integrate guided meditation, scripting, and emotional anchoring into a single routine:

1. **Morning Meditation:** Begin your day with a guided meditation to visualize your goal and feel its emotional resonance.
2. **Midday Scripting:** Spend time writing a detailed script about your desired reality, reinforcing your connection to your goal.
3. **Emotional Anchor Activation:** Use your anchor gesture throughout the day to maintain high-vibration emotions and alignment.

Case Studies: Recognizing Opportunities

Case Study 1: Career Synchronicity

Scenario: Rachel wanted to start her own photography business but wasn't sure where to begin.

Opportunity: While talking to a friend, Rachel casually mentioned her passion for photography. Her friend introduced her to someone seeking a photographer for an upcoming event.

Result: Rachel took the job, which led to referrals and the eventual launch of her business.

Lesson: Sharing your intentions with others can create unexpected opportunities.

Case Study 2: Health and Wellness Insight

Scenario: Marco wanted to improve his fitness but struggled with motivation.

Opportunity: He kept seeing ads for a local yoga studio and finally decided to attend a class. The supportive community and regular practice inspired him to adopt healthier habits overall.

Result: Marco not only improved his fitness but also discovered a passion for yoga.

Lesson: Pay attention to recurring signs and explore them, even if they seem small.

Conclusion

Congratulations on completing *7 Days to Master Manifesting with Project 369, Law of Attraction, and Angel Numbers: Where the Power of Thought Meets Infinite Possibilities*. This is more than just the end of a book—it's the beginning of your transformation into a powerful co-creator of your reality. Over the past chapters, you've explored the principles of manifestation, harnessed the power of thoughts, emotions, and actions, and integrated advanced techniques to expand your potential. Now, it's time to take these insights and make them a part of your life.

The Path Forward: Your Infinite Possibilities

Manifestation is not a one-time act but an ongoing practice of aligning your energy with your desires. Each step you've taken in this 7-day journey builds a foundation for greater awareness, intentionality, and fulfillment. By incorporating the techniques you've learned into your daily life, you can continue to attract abundance, joy, and growth in every area of your life.

- **Trust the Process:** Even after completing the program, remember that patience and faith are key. The universe is always working behind the scenes to bring your desires to life.
- **Stay Consistent:** Revisit the practices from the 7-day program whenever you feel the need to refocus or recharge your energy.
- **Celebrate Your Progress:** Acknowledge every synchronicity, success, and lesson as proof that you are on the right path.

What's Next?

Your journey doesn't end here. To help you stay inspired and supported, I encourage you to explore these additional resources and tools:

1. **More from Izumi Nagi Publications:**
   - Dive deeper into topics like the Law of Attraction, advanced manifestation techniques, and self-discovery with other books and guides from Izumi Nagi Publications. Each title is designed to empower you on your journey to infinite possibilities.
2. **Angel Number Guidebook:**
   - Scan the QR code at the beginning of this book to download a comprehensive PDF with detailed meanings of angel numbers. Learn how to interpret these divine messages and align with their guidance in your everyday life.
3. **Printable Templates for Daily Manifestation Tracking:**
   - Use the printable templates provided via the QR code to track your affirmations, progress, and reflections during the 7-day program. These tools are designed to keep you organized and focused on your goals.

A Final Thought: You Are the Creator

The greatest lesson of this book is that the power to manifest lies within you. Every thought you think, every emotion you feel, and every action you take contributes to the reality you create. By embracing this truth and practicing the principles of Project 369, the Law of Attraction, and angel numbers, you hold the key to unlocking infinite possibilities.

Stay Connected

- **Join the Community:** Share your success stories, challenges, and insights with like-minded individuals. Look for online groups, forums, or social media spaces that discuss Project 369 and manifestation practices.

- **Leave a Review:** If you've enjoyed this book, consider leaving a review to help others discover it and begin their own transformation journey.

Thank you for allowing *Izumi Nagi Publications* to be part of your manifestation journey. Remember, the universe is always listening, and the possibilities are truly endless. The next step is yours to take.

Let the magic of manifestation guide you toward your dreams, one thought, one emotion, and one action at a time.

With gratitude and infinite possibilities,

Izumi Nagi Publications

Discover the Ultimate
ANGEL NUMBERS *Guide*

Over **50** Pages of Insight and Guidance!

Scan the QR code to download your exclusive **Angel Numbers Guide**. Discover the meanings behind divine patterns and learn how to align with their guidance to manifest your dreams. Don't miss this powerful resource!

Your journey to clarity and transformation starts here!

Stay Focused and Organized on Your Manifestation Journey!

Scan the QR code to download your Printable Templates for Daily Manifestation Tracking.

These tools are designed to help you:

- Track your affirmations morning, afternoon, and evening.
- Monitor your progress throughout the 7-day program.
- Reflect on your daily thoughts, actions, and results.

Take the first step toward manifesting your dreams with clarity and purpose!

Printed in Dunstable, United Kingdom